In the Course of a Dream
EMANUEL FOR LOVE

In the Course of a Dream
EMANUEL FOR LOVE
Copyright © Ruben Bailey 2007
Penny For My Thought
Washington, DC

All Rights Reserved. No part of this book may be reproduced in any form or by any electronic or mechanical means including information storage and retrieval systems without written permission from the publisher, except by reviewers who may quote brief passages to be printed in a magazine, newspaper or book review.

ISBN: 978-0-6151-5178-6

www.pennyformythought.org
emanuelforlove@pennyformythought.org

Cover Design by Leah Riley
Manuscript Editing by Sal Rachele

Spirituality is a treasure

to live for all humanity,

to overcome a notion,

in a time when spirits rejoice.

Special thanks to my editor Sal Rachale. Thanks Sal!

Above all else...Thank You GOD!

In Loving Memory Of

Daniel Osorio

My Best Friend

Who Died of AIDS On

January 10, 1995

In the Course of a Dream
EMANUEL FOR LOVE

By Ruben Bailey

The picture of me on the cover was taken in the winter of 1989 in Pittsburgh, Pennsylvania. I had just moved away from California, my home, to follow my dream. At that time my dream was simple -- to live where it snowed. This was my first fallen snow. I took a handful of snow, molded it into a little ball and tossed it into the air to watch it fall. My partner Michael captured the image on film. I was in awe to finally be living my dream, living in a city where I could experience snowfall. It was my dream come true.

The picture surfaced one day when I was looking for suitable cover art for the book. Looking back I can say this is where it all began. My little dream has grown. It is with the same awe and reverence that I have gathered my dreams into the little snowball that is this book to bring together what is rightfully beyond words. The picture seemed to capture the essence and feeling behind my inspiration. Little did I know then how God was planning on using me to help carry forth the Divine Plan and help humanity awaken to the Dream.

CONTENTS

Prelude to the Reader	i
The Book	1
The Calling	11
Fear - The Battle Within	37
Wrestling with Demons	65
Angels and Spirit Guides	79
God The Observer and Master Dreamer	105
Inter-Dimensional Living	119
Right Living	143
The Higher Self	161
It's a Miracle; High on Life	183
The Land of Canaan	205

"And he said, Hear my words: If there is a prophet among you, I the Lord make myself known to him in a vision, I speak with him in a dream."

Numbers 12:6

Prelude to the Reader

I have purposefully stayed away from providing too much dream interpretation. My objective was not to have a "how to" on dream analysis so that my life could be psychoanalyzed. I want it to remain an "experience" that people will crave. This is something you must want for yourself. It is about effectuating your awakening. It must be felt with the heart and not intellectualized too much. Passion is what drives the awakening. To peg the dreams to particulars in my life and logically analyze what is a multi-dimensional experience is to flatten it like a tortilla. Being Hispanic, I love tortillas but tortillas will not serve me here. Loosen up, open your mind and your heart and allow spirit to flow. Let go of all the notions upon which you have based your existence. Nothing is what you expect it to be.

Heaven is a place where very few words are spoken. There is a reason why spirits communicate telepathically, because often what needs to be expressed cannot be said in words. Telepathic communication comes with feeling, imagery and a sense of knowing. I could never give justice to a multi-dimensional experience in any dream interpretation. This is why no one can interpret a dream for you except the dreamer.

I need this dough to rise. I want to make spiritual bread, not tortillas; leavened manna for the soul. I want my readers to stay within the dream experience. It is not about Ruben, it is about humanity. Please do not get caught up in my life; otherwise you risk losing the message.

We are all part of and have full access to the Universal Mind of God. Because of this, you already know me. You are a part of me and I am a part of you. What I have experienced will have meaning to you if you allow yourself to find it because you are in the world and we are part of the same system.

IN THE COURSE OF A DREAM EMANUEL FOR LOVE

Our native language is the Feng Shui of symbols. It is your language of origin. You know this language in your heart. It is universal in origin. All you have to do is reacquaint yourself with it. Observe yourself, the symbols and the patterns around you, the interplay. As you become aware, synchronicity will show up in all areas of your life as the pennies did in mine. This will let you know you are on the right track to becoming aware of who you are and the powers of creation that you possess.

The voice of the Holy Spirit is the Dream and the Holy Spirit is your Higher Self, just as you are One with God. You exist within The Master Dream. Your sandbox is your individual dreams where you lay the blueprint and foundation for the things that come into manifestation in your life. The dream is the precursor of physical manifestation. To understand the dream is to understand why we are in the situations we are in. We have divine direction in creating heaven right where we find ourselves.

We drive this creation of physical reality while headless because we are not conscious of the dream. We have no idea how other dimensions are affecting this one and we make no use of the wealth of assistance that is out there in the unseen realms. How much better would our lives be if we were fully aware? We must step outside ourselves to become one with the Observer, our Higher Self, to truly become active participants in this dream. We must be driven by our True Purpose. Manifestation driven without the awareness and guidance of our Higher Self will only fail us in the end. The essence of Love must be present in everything we do in order to bring about true and lasting happiness because that is who we are.

I am Christian but I have also fully embraced all of the great spiritual teachers of every major religion. Religion is like the shell that protects the embryo. It serves its purpose, but once you have come of age there is no need

PRELUDE TO THE READER

to carry the shell around with you, for you will find the Word written in your heart. I do, however, encourage everyone to expand their knowledge of scripture from all parts of the world and from every culture. God is a beautiful thing if beheld with an open mind and an open heart. Make no mistake; God has full expression in all of creation. There is not a stone that I have yet to upturn where I have not found God.

Many answers I do not have, I simply know them in my heart. My soul is wrapped up in the pages of this book. It is with an immense love for humanity and a true desire of my heart to see you achieve oneness that I deliver this message of hope and good wishes for a brighter and peaceful future.

My question to you is, are you ready to come of age?

The Book

The Theatre of Life

I must have died and gone to heaven. My dreams tonight were the most spectacular I have ever had. This dream/vision was truly in living color. I feel like I was not only allowed into the theatre but also allowed back-stage privileges to experience the most incredible journey of a man's life. The cinematography was phenomenal. This one is truly an epic.

I woke myself up suddenly in the middle of the night with a forceful, angry and extremely loud cry from within, "GET OUT OF HERE!" I was astonished. Where did that come from? I felt like I had just been exorcised as in the Exorcist. Feeling safe again, I closed my eyes and saw a vision. I saw what looked like God in the heavens tossing a book across the sea. The book landed on a desk where a man sat. The pages of the book flung open upon hitting the desk. I then saw the man reach for a pen and begin writing in the book.

I slowly began to doze off while fighting hard to maintain my remembrance. With a mind of its own on automatic reflex, my hand suddenly but gently hit my face as if someone had lifted my arm and pushed my hand into my face to tell me to pay attention and stay conscious. I immediately thought to myself, "Huh, that's probably how you spirits keep waking me up night after night to get my attention." I then remained conscious just relaxing, waiting to see what my attention was being called to see.

IN THE COURSE OF A DREAM EMANUEL FOR LOVE

Time went by and I must have lost whatever thoughts were in my head. I laid there watching TV. It appeared to be the evening news anchored by two women. They were reading from a book. The volume was apparently turned down on the television because I could see their mouths moving but I could not hear any audio. It then occurred to me—"Wait a minute, dummy, it's the middle of the night and your eyes are closed. Besides, you never watch TV. Why would you be watching it at this hour of the night? You must be watching some kind of dream vision. You are experiencing the dream at 100% lucidity. Now is your chance. You have arrived."

This was unlike any vision or dream I had ever had. The difference was that what I was seeing with closed eyes was in living color, FULL LIVING COLOR WITH PERFECT CLARITY. I remained relaxed so as to not lose this altered state of consciousness.

Who were these two women and what in God's name were they reading to me and why couldn't I hear them? Maybe on some level I understood what they were reading to me. I was simply beside myself. All visions I had had to date had been in a single color scale, usually blue. I watched these two women read from the book for what seemed like an eternity. The script they read was very long. I knew I dared not move and lose the reception on this station within my mind. As luck would have it I got an itch on my nose, which I tried hard not to scratch. Then my forehead itched and I tried not to scratch it, then my neck itched. By this time, I could not hold out any longer. I had to scratch, and OH MY GOD, it felt so good to scratch.

As I suspected, the image of the women began to fade in and out. I tried to hold the reception steady but I was losing the signal until finally all I could see was a myriad of rainbow colors, beautiful rainbow colors. The colors were so beautiful I did not want to lose my lucid awareness so I remained with the colored lights. This went on for a while. I thought this could go on forever but I didn't care. I wanted to experience it.

I then started to dream. I was with my family and we were playing hide and seek. We all hid in the bushes and camouflaged ourselves. Our father came around to look for us and he was unable to see the others. Unlike the others, my camouflage was only partial as I was only now learning how to camouflage and play hide and seek. My father saw me hiding in the bushes. He looked right at me and said in a playful and jovial way, "Oh, there is Ruben." We continued playing and we hid in other places. My cousins were hiding in the trees and were making a cooing sound. It was so funny because everyone thought they were real animals cooing but I knew they were in fact my cousins. You could not distinguish them from nature. It was all very natural.

I was told to take care of my little brother. He was given a brown puppy that was so cute and adorable. Benji wanted the keys to the house but I told him that I was tasked to safeguard them for him and that I would be responsible for the keys. I told little Benji that he could have the keys when he grew older and more mature and could assume responsibility for himself.

There was another young man in his early 20's playing with us who was wearing a red shirt and white shorts. He paused to tie his shoe laces and said he had to run to the restroom. He said that the game was a lot of fun but he really wanted to get high. Apparently, he was an addict in recovery, yet he still wanted nothing more than to get high. He told me he had a wife. "A wife? How could you have a wife if you are gay?" I asked. To this he replied, "I have a wife and I like to get high."

Still 100% lucid and visioning, I realized spirit energy is all around us camouflaged to appear as nature, for which our cousins the angels and faeries are responsible. We are engaged in a clever game of hide and seek.

IN THE COURSE OF A DREAM EMANUEL FOR LOVE

Marriage to a wife does not represent anyone other than the Higher Self or "big brother" in whose care we rest. I am married to my Higher Self. We all have that special Love relationship with God and all of creation. I realized that all the veiled or camouflaged images I had been seeing in visions were in fact God's creation, and his creation extends well beyond man. I was now seeing what God created for what it really is. My Higher Self maintains the keys to the kingdom and the inherent power of creation that goes along with possessing those keys until such time that I have matured in the game of hide and seek.

I was shown the stage of life where "All That Is" is acted out. I could see the stage and the curtain or veil of separation. I then found myself in my bed within the theatre of life and a great wind came along and lifted my bed. It blew the stage curtain wide open and I saw the sea of consciousness that lies just beyond the veil. The wind carried my bed in flight and I sailed past the curtain and out over the ocean waters. I could see the turquoise sea and the many waves upon the ocean. Grey clouds were up ahead but the sea was fresh and clear. It had an invigorating and brisk feel to it, like the chill of an autumn morning. I saw individual vessels upon the ocean charting their course on previously uncharted waters. I was not the only one upon this sea.

It was incredibly surreal. How was it that I was seeing all this through the mind's eye? I heard the voice of my sister say, "You are like the phoenix who flies out ahead of man to survey the land and report back what you see and hear so that others may safely follow and see for themselves." A wave of calm swept over my body and I knew I had arrived. As I sensed the dream/vision ending, I heard a voice from above say, "Thank You."

THE BOOK

Thank You, Lord, for blessing me with a spiritual high that is beyond that which words can describe. I am addicted to love. Help me today, Lord, to remain on course in service to you. Today brings a new beginning for all mankind.

EMANUEL FOR LOVE

God is with us (a Manual for Love)

The alarm clock rang this morning and as usual I promptly hit the snooze button and closed my eyes to meditate. I then saw letters begin to appear in a vision. I could see a written message appearing before my eyes. A thick blanket of fog covered the letters. If this was a message from the Heavens, I needed to come in for a closer look to make out what the letters said to ascertain the meaning of the vision. As the fog began to clear, I saw that the letters were embossed upon the cover of a bound book. These letters comprised the title of a book. The letters were equally spaced, making it difficult to read. As I strained to see clearly, I read each letter one by one.

The letters read:

"E M A N U E L F O R L O V E"

I could clearly make out the last four letters being LOVE. I kept trying to sound it out--emanuelforlove, e man u e l for Love, e Manuel for Love. Ah ha! I got it, but why is "A Manual for Love" spelled with E's instead of A's? What is wrong with my perception? How could I have confused E's for A's? It then dawned on me that the title of the book had a double meaning. Therein lies the irony. The E's were intentional. This was a message from Emmanuel, intended to be *a Manual for Love*. I quickly ran downstairs to do a quick search for all Biblical references to Emmanuel.

> "*¹⁸Now the birth of Jesus Christ was on this wise: When as his mother Mary was espoused to Joseph, before they came together, she was found with child of the Holy Ghost.*
>
> *¹⁹Then Joseph her husband, being a just man, and not willing to make her a public example, was minded to put her away privily.*
>
> *²⁰But while he thought on these things, behold, the angel of the LORD appeared unto him in a dream, saying, Joseph, thou son of David, fear not to take unto thee Mary thy wife: for that which is conceived in her is of the Holy Ghost.*
>
> *²¹And she shall bring forth a son, and thou shalt call his name JESUS: for he shall save his people from their sins.*
>
> *²²Now all this was done, that it might be fulfilled which was spoken of the Lord by the prophet, saying,*
>
> *²³Behold, a virgin shall be with child, and shall bring forth a son, and they shall call his name Emmanuel, which being interpreted is, God with us.*
>
> *²⁴Then Joseph being raised from sleep did as the angel of the Lord had bidden him, and took unto him his wife:*
>
> *²⁵And knew her not till she had brought forth her firstborn son: and he called his name JESUS.*" (Matthew 1:18-25 KJV)

THE BOOK

How many times have I read that passage at Christmas time and glossed over the fact that the angel that came to announce the birth of Christ came to Joseph by way of a dream. God uses dreams to deliver messages to us and now is no exception. His word, which is written in our hearts, has been staring us in the face night after night and we have failed to bring his comfort back with us and apply it in our daily lives.

This aroused my curiosity and I went on a biblical search for every reference that had to do with dreams. I was astonished at how many references I found. Did you know the entire Book of Revelation is based on the dreams of one man and is thought to be an interpretation of the Book of Daniel who himself was not only a prophet but a dreamer?

> *"And he said, Hear my words: If there is a prophet among you, I the Lord make myself known to him in a vision, I speak with him in a dream."* (Numbers 12:6)

The Battle between the Beast and the Lion, Pages of a Book yet Unwritten

Early this morning, I had a dream in which *I find myself reading a book. I am so engrossed in the book that the story comes to life all around me and I become the main character of the book. I am running from a mythological beast. The beast corners me in a barn and I am in utter fear and panic. I must free myself and escape.*

My remembrance comes back to remind me that I am simply reliving a story told in a book and there is really nothing here for me to fear. At this point, a great lion comes in and stands between me and the beast to protect me and intercede on my behalf. The beast and the lion wrestle with each other as I take the opportunity and run for safety. The beast is much larger than the lion but the lion has courage and stands firm against the beast. Looking for refuge, I turn and notice a golden ray of light coming into the barn through a slit in one of the walls. I decide to pry my way through the narrow opening. As I do, golden rays of light come streaming in and something magical happens. The barn is filled with golden light and the beast and the barn begin to magically disappear and fade away. All that remains is me and the lion on a canvas of white. The lion has defeated the beast.

In the climax, I become fully lucid standing there with the book in hand and staring at the lion. I know I must gather as much information as possible while in this lucid state so I can bring it back. I know this book I am holding contains the key to unlocking the mysteries of my life and will advance me forward according to my divine right.

I quickly examine the book cover, which is dark green, and notice it has an ornate seal denoting its authenticity. I then examine the pages of the book and notice that it is written in various languages. I recognize some sections written in Spanish, some in French and some in Aramaic. I am trying hard to commit something, anything to memory. I decide to turn to the final pages of the book to see if I can determine how the story ends. The final chapters of the book have an inner seal which magically rotates like a revolving door as I gaze upon it. The pages open magically revealing the final chapters of the book. The writing upon these final pages appears to be encrypted the way computer passwords are, with each letter appearing as black diamonds on the page.

I thought to myself, what an amazing experience it is to pause the dream and become fully lucid to consciously page through my book of life. I

The Book

lay my head back to take in the feeling of sheer ecstasy and utter bliss, when at that moment my consciousness began to float away, ascending into the heavens above. I lost feeling with any part of my body. I suddenly felt detached. I was pure consciousness and completely free.

I then realized I was awake and floating above my body. I could see everything with perfect and vivid clarity as I witnessed everything through my third eye. I began to pay attention to where I was. I was floating above my house and I could see my red truck below me as I floated higher and higher. I was whisked across the skies so high that I felt I was somewhere circling the earth. The euphoria was incredible. As if on a rollercoaster ride, I began circling the earth at a tremendous speed. I sped across the earth until I came to a lake. The lake was reflecting the light of the moon, which was high in the sky. I could see a man standing on a boat that was docked along the bank of the lake. The man looked up at me and began shaking his head and waving. He grabbed what looked like a mirror and held it in his left hand and began reflecting the light back at me so as to get my attention like an SOS. I somehow felt that the light he was reflecting was not that of the moon but instead, the light of my soul floating above his boat. What I experienced was nothing other than nirvana.

I then opened my eyes and I was back in my body lying in my bed. Not wanting to give up the vision, I closed my eyes again and as if I had turned my inner TV back on, I then saw clear as day an older woman standing alongside a horse drawn carriage. All about the woman were creamy clouds with yellow rays of light. Her face was pure white. She had come to welcome me home. Then another horse drawn carriage pulled up beside her and yet another angelic figure stepped out to greet and welcome me home.

IN THE COURSE OF A DREAM EMANUEL FOR LOVE

I opened my eyes again and looked at my bed sheet thinking no one would ever believe this. How blessed I am. I had to find a way to share this experience with everyone. If I could experience divine bliss, anyone can. This must be why God is calling me to write this book, to share with mankind the process I followed that brought about my spiritual awakening.

The Calling

A Measure of Wheat for a Penny

> *"And I heard a voice in the midst of the four beasts say, A measure of wheat for a penny, and three measures of barley for a penny; and see thou hurt not the oil and the wine."* (Revelation 6:6 KJV)

For me, all the magic has revolved around a single penny--a wheat penny. It began in the fall of 1995 with a series of precognitive dreams. I had been seeing a therapist who suggested that I journal my dreams to help me get in touch with a host of unresolved issues. I felt very much an outcast. I was poor, Hispanic, gay, and HIV positive.

I desperately wanted to reconcile my life to God. My best friend had just passed away from AIDS and I did not want to die without coming to know God. The precognitive dreams concerned a book that ironically my therapist had also asked me to read. The book was *"Iron John, A Book about Men"*, by Robert Bly. For the last three chapters of the book, I would dream the night before about chapters in the book I had yet to read. How is it that I knew the story line of the last three chapters in the book before ever having set my eyes upon those pages? Information that seemed at first to be meaningless hooked my interest and forced me to look around and ask, "Is someone or something out there, or is God trying to get my attention?"

The answer came in a subsequent dream. This dream is the hallmark of all the dreams in my life. It led me to know there is a God setting everything into motion guiding my path toward self-actualization and revealing my purpose in life.

Dream: Wait One Cent (October 15, 1995)

I am working at an elementary school servicing the lunch lines for the kids. I usually eat my lunch before their lunch hour begins but today I do not have a meal ticket. The supervisor of the cafeteria tells me that she has an extra meal ticket that I can have but before I can have it, I must agree to pick up all the pennies that have fallen on the ground. I agree and proceed to get down on my knees to collect the fallen pennies. There are so many pennies that I cannot hold them all in my hands. They begin falling out of my hands. I am trying hard not to drop any while at the same time picking up the remaining pennies that are still on the ground. I am anxious because I want to get my food before it is too late. I finally get to the last penny and I notice it looks different from all the others. It is a very old penny with much wear on it. As I pick it up and look closely, I realize that it is a wheat penny.

The next day after I finished reading *"Iron John",* I decided to stop after work at Borders Bookstore to buy another book. At the suggestion of my therapist, I purchased, *"Fire in the Belly, A Book about Being a Man"*, by Sam Keen. As I walked out of the store, I quickly took the book out of the bag to page through it. Standing in front of Borders Books, I suddenly had a very strange feeling of déjà vu, except I could not pinpoint what it was that I had already seen or experienced. Puzzled, I scratched my head and looked around to try to piece the puzzle together. My eyes then fell to my feet and to my total disbelief I found myself standing in the middle of a bunch of pennies that someone had apparently dropped on the ground. Memory of the dream immediately came rushing back into my mind. There were no nickels, dimes or quarters; only a bunch of pennies. I could not believe it.

This was apparently just another manifestation in a series of precognitive dreams. I knew God had to be at work here. I just did not understand what he was trying to tell me. Remembering the dream and knowing I had agreed to pick up the pennies, I got down on my knees to collect the fallen pennies. One by one I picked them up. Would the last penny in fact be a wheat penny? I just knew in my heart that it had to be true. I had called on God and this was God's way of answering. This was about a dream come true. In my mind I prayed, "God, if there is something you want me to do, Lord, please make it clear to me now."

There were dozens of pennies. When I came to the last penny, I paused, not knowing what to expect. Were the heavens going to open up? Was I going to hear God's voice? Would an angel appear in front of me? Since it was already nightfall, I picked up the last penny and stood up and walked over to the window display of the bookstore to have a close look at this miracle penny. Upon examination and to my amazement the penny was in fact a wheat penny.

I felt overwhelming joy and peace in knowing God was really out there. On the other hand, I still had no clue what he was trying to tell me. I had a great sense of frustration come over me in not knowing what was being asked of me. "What do you want me to do?" All my energy drained from my body and I just stood there with my body and head pressed up against the bookstore display window. With my eyes closed and tears of frustration running down my face, I called out to God, "Please God, what is it you want me to do?" Nothing. I heard no voice, I saw no divine apparition, nothing.

"Whatever, let's go," I heard my ego say to me. I wiped my tears and as I opened my eyes and regained my composure, it suddenly hit me. The answer was staring me in the face. I could practically hear God's voice saying, "I want you to write a book."

This book is the fulfillment of that request.

The saying, "Pennies from Heaven", took on a personal meaning for me and dream journaling became my connection to God. For the next 10 years, God would confirm his lessons in my external world with synchronicity by placing pennies in my path for me to find at precisely the right place and time. The synchronicity of the pennies became unmistakably God's voice. Interestingly enough I always found pennies in groups of ones or threes and I knew God in His own way was winking at me letting me know that I was on the right track.

For those 10 years not much happened; I did my dream work and studied anything and everything I could get my hands on: Buddhism, Hinduism, Taoism, Edgar Cayce, Self Realization Fellowship, philosophy, mysticism and mythology. Having been raised Catholic, and being gay, I really did not have a good taste for Christianity. However, with the sense that God really cared about me, I wanted to give Christianity another try and study it for myself instead of relying on what others had to say. Therefore, I renewed my interest in Christianity and began studying the Bible independently and with different Christian denominations, including the Mormons. Of course, as soon as I told them I was gay, they all wanted me to renounce my so-called lifestyle choice and be baptized. Since I would not do that, they eventually wrote me off as a lost soul and went about their business. However, I knew that God had not

The Calling

abandoned me; he was with me. I persisted in my independent study and eventually found a non-denominational Christian church that did accept me. I was baptized by them since I felt baptism into the Catholic faith was not my conscious choice as an infant.

Things finally began to shift into high gear in the summer of 2005. I began to see with my eyes closed, colored lights panning back and forth in my field of vision when I was falling asleep at night. Trying to find the cause of these lights, I researched the Internet and found instances where terminally ill patients often reported having mystical experiences similar to mine several months before dying. Was I having a mystical experience? More importantly, was I nearing my own death? In November of that year, I took a trip to visit my parents in California. While on that trip one day my sister and I were talking and out of the blue she shared with me that she had this synchronistic thing happening with finding pennies. She had never shared her penny experiences with me and I never thought to share mine with her. We looked at each other in disbelief. I also shared with her my mystical experience of seeing the colored lights. I affectionately termed the experience "my night lights".

I took this coincidence to be a sign from God signaling me to put pen to paper or fingertips to keyboard and began the actual writing process for the book He had wanted me to write. I still did not know what God wanted me to write about, but I assumed it had to do with my life experience and dream work as a source of divine guidance.

That trip was full of synchronicities but now the synchronicities were shared between me, my sister and the universe. Suddenly the phenomenon involved a person outside of me. We were like kids in a candy store. My sister and I began talking almost every day.

Wait For Me! I Was Given a Second Chance

My life had been anything but picture perfect. It was with great pain that I sat and began to write this section of my life, but it needed to come out because I needed to be released from the pain I had carried in my soul. My whole life was a struggle to fit in and feel worthy. There were times in my life where I did not feel I had anything to live for. Poor, Hispanic and gay was only where it began. I always felt like I was an after-thought in my mother's life because she gave birth to me when she was 38. I was embarrassed of her because she was so much older than all the other mothers of my childhood friends. I was embarrassed of my father because he was the neighborhood alcoholic whom the children made fun of every night when he would be laid up in the streets trying to stumble his way home from a drunken stupor.

My mother cleaned houses for a living and my father washed dishes in a local restaurant and sold popsicles on the street corners. Neither of my parents spoke a word of English. I would grow up to be a sex addict and drug addict. I did not understand why God was trying to communicate with me. Didn't he know that I was condemned to go to hell? The biggest question I had struggled with was, "Why are you calling upon me?"

I had tried to live a good life within the circumstances to which I was born, but eventually the pain of life was always greater and I found myself back in my addictive behavior patterns trying to feel good about myself or "fit in" in some way.

I was a functional addict but an addict nonetheless and in just as much pain. Shortly after returning home from my trip to California, I began having problems in my relationship with my partner of six years, and I fell into deep depression and anxiety. My world was falling apart. My partner was also struggling with his own addictions, which were expressed in very abusive ways. I lived with verbal abuse and disrespect similar to the way my father had treated my mother, and I could not allow myself to fall into the hands of a verbally abusive and disrespectful partner. On top of this, we were knee deep in debt because of my partner's outlandish spending required to uphold his image. I felt I had to stay in the relationship because I could not afford to make payments on all the credit card debt that we held together. I was having frequent panic attacks and low blood sugar where I was passing out regularly.

One day I passed out while driving my car to work. I woke up in the lanes of oncoming traffic with people honking at me. Three days after Thanksgiving, after partying and living to excess and not taking care of myself, my sugar level crashed, causing me to have a grand mal seizure where I collapsed and became incontinent. I lost consciousness. My partner called the paramedics who came and rushed me to the emergency room.

I woke up in the ambulance, not knowing what had happened to me. God temporarily hid from me the details of my near-death experience but it was later revealed to me in a vision. Something happened that day that changed my awareness forever. Suddenly, I was able to see spirits. When I woke up I didn't know if I were alive or dead. I felt like I was present in both the here and now and the afterlife. I was freaked out, to say the least. In the hospital I could not tell the difference between spirits present and the hospital workers.

The night lights intensified and I began seeing visions. In one vision I was shown what had happened to me and how I was held accountable for my life. I could see the paramedics struggling to get my vital signs. I could not believe I was seeing myself. I stared into my own eyes in disbelief and as I beheld them I could see the life force slowly leaving my body and my vital signs flat lining. Everyone gave a collective sigh and I had the sense that I had died needlessly. A man in a white gown then turned to me in spirit and asked me to look at what I had done with my life. On the table was a withered forearm. The sight of the forearm was so incredibly painful that I could not bear to look upon it. Then in the background I head a voice say, "Wait." I turned back and down below I could see the hospital workers rushing to assist me, crying out, "He's back, he's back!"

They quickly moved my body onto another stretcher and wheeled me away. As my body was wheeled past my consciousness, my body's eyes looked up at me and said "Wait for me! Please wait for me! I was given a second chance."

Everything went dark with the exception of a beacon of light in the distance. Its core was pure white with blue rays emanating from it in all directions. I moved toward the light to see once and for all the source of this light. As I approached, my eyes beheld a circle of angels. They stood in radiant white robes standing in a circle with their head back, their wings outstretched and their backs fully arched. They were looking intently upon something above them in the heavens. Now curious, I followed their gaze and ascended to the next level and there was another circle of angels with their heads back looking up into the heavens with their wings outstretched and their backs arched. Again I followed their gaze and ascended yet another level to find yet another circle of angels. These were concentric ascending circles of angels.

As I ascended higher and higher I found circle upon circle of ascending angels until I reached the center where I came upon a mount where two women were in prayer kneeling. They had white veils over their heads that draped to touch the ground upon which they were kneeling. Just beyond them a top a mount was Christ upon the cross. Light emanated from his spiritual body. My heart stopped and I could not believe that I, a simple man, was blessed to

The Calling

behold such an image. The amount of light that radiated from the cross was very intense. I then realized these angels were in this posture trying to absorb as much light from Christ as possible, like a daisy in the sun. To this day, the light has not left me and I now know that it is the light of Christ emanating from the cross that I see and recognize as my night lights. I see them in meditation and as I am falling asleep. I know my life today to be a blessing, a second chance at making a difference in the world.

My dream experiences following the incident intensified greatly. I would often be awoken at night suddenly from a dream to find the dream images standing in my bedroom or floating above my bed. I would often hear voices in my head. For a while, I thought the seizure had caused brain damage or I was losing my mind. I started seeing a psychiatrist and a therapist again. I was prescribed anti-depressants and anti-psychotic drugs in addition to having to monitor my glucose levels and take HIV meds. I also made a commitment to myself to refrain from any consumption of alcohol or non-prescription drugs. If I had been given a second chance, I needed to find a better way to live. If I were going to save my relationship, I had to have the courage to set an example and change my life. In the end my partner tried to stop his own chaos, but the lifestyle to which he was addicted proved itself more important and we parted ways.

A part of me wondered if maybe, just maybe, the spirits I was seeing and voices in my head might in fact be real. Nah! It couldn't be true. Yet, I had an incessant inner prodding to know the truth. I knew of only one thing I could turn to for comfort and guidance. I knew it was time to start writing because what I was experiencing had purpose. It would prove to be the material for this book. I renewed the commitment to my dream journaling and analysis but this time, I would journal my dreams on the computer just in case I wanted to use any of them as examples in the book. I also purchased a digital voice recorder to make it easier for me to capture as much detail as possible from my dreams and to analyze and look for hidden messages from spirit.

I soon crossed over into a new and deeper level in my dream experience. The nightly awakenings continued with greater frequency. Spirits would awaken me to deliver messages telepathically. I would grab my voice recorder, which I always maintained beside my bed, and capture any and all details I could remember. I would then meditate until I fell back to sleep. This pattern of sudden awakening, capturing the dream and mediating became an every night occurrence. As with any skill, over time I got better and better at it to the point where I could literally enter the dream state while fully awake. Few achieve this state. I learned there is a name for it. It is called WILD, Wakefully Induced Lucid Dreaming, and I can tell you it is absolutely wild; a virtual reality like no other where your consciousness is totally free from the body.

Knock! Knock! Michael, Open the Door

I awoke in the morning to the sound of someone knocking at my front door. A voice said, "Michael, open the door. Michael, open the door, I just want to talk to you."

"Who's that," I thought? Who could be knocking on my front door looking for someone named Michael? There was no Michael living here so I assumed it had to be next door. I gave it no thought and closed my eyes and laid back down.

The Calling

Once again I heard knocking. "Michael, open the door, we just want to talk to you." Again I opened my eyes, thinking it sounded like the knocking was coming from inside my house. I listened carefully but did not hear anything so once again I laid back down and began my normal mediation. I immediately went into a vision, where I could see my bedroom in this vision. I could see through the bedroom walls at what looked like dozens of police officers and a bearded man in a robe standing at the other side of my bedroom door knocking. Here was the man that had been knocking all along.

The knocking was coming from within me. Once again, I heard him knock and cry out to me, "Michael, please open the door, we just want to talk to you."

The knocking was definitely coming from within me. I immediately thought, "What have I done wrong? Why are they trying to arrest me and who is this bearded man? Did he mistake me for someone else or did he just get my name wrong? My name is not Michael."

Yet the knocking was coming from within me. Knowing it was just in my mind, I remained calm and quietly scanned the room within the vision to see if anything was out of the norm. The police officers and the bearded man appeared as moonstruck images, like shadows. I could see them but they could not see me. I saw the police officer at the door knock and yell out again, "Michael, answer the door, I just want to talk to you."

There was no doubt it was me they were looking for. I sat up in my bed, opened my eyes and said, "I'm here, I'm here!"

I wanted to open the door, but *what* door? Where *is* this door? I saw nothing so I laid back down to fall asleep again. As soon as I closed my eyes I returned to the vision. Once again the moonstruck officers were at my door within me. This time, I kept my eyes closed and sat up within the vision. I calmly said to them, "I'm here, I'm here." They immediately saw me and I could see their rifles pointed at me.

I thought, Oh shit, what did I just do? I gave my cover away. Now they have spotted me and they are probably going to arrest me. I could vaguely see through their veiled faces, such that I could make out some of their facial features. Frightened, I opened my eyes and sat up again. I then thought, "What are you afraid of, Michael?" Michael?? Why did I just call myself Michael? Then I heard a voice from within say, "God is with you." Reassured, I told myself I have nothing, absolutely nothing, to fear. I then closed my eyes again and as soon as I closed them I had a false awakening.

Outside my second floor window, I see police officers. I turn to Joe and say, "They've come for me. You better let them in now. I can't hide anymore."

It then occurs to me that Joe and I separated some time ago and we have not been together in quite some time, so this has to be a false awakening. I know I am still within the dream vision though my surroundings appear identical to my real bedroom.

I see the officers now coming in through the window. They all have veiled faces like no police squad I have ever seen. At this point all my fears are gone because I know it is a dream. They are coming in through the window furthest from where my bed is. I turn to look around and observe my surroundings. I notice one thing that is out of order. All my window shades are bamboo as expected, except for the one window closest to me which has a white sheer curtain. I look through the white sheer curtain and notice the earth in the background. I sit up in my dream bed and move closer to the window. I can see that the earth is moving. The earth outside me is in flight.

I think, "WHAT?" I open the shade to get a better look and find myself on the other side of the window. I then notice that the police officers are not police officers at all but

The Calling

angels. *Their police hats are not hats but hallows and their machine guns they are wearing on their backs are not machine guns but wings.*

What I am seeing are my fears projected upon their moonstruck silhouettes. I realize I have been afraid of their shadows all along. I then look back at the earth around me and it is pristine and beautiful. It feels like I am on a newly formed planet where all life is vibrant and teaming in its youth. I realize then how old and worn out our earth is in waking life. This dream vision is vibrant as no other place I have ever seen. The sun is so magnificently bright.

I then find myself flying among a flock of silver glistening birds. They are so shiny and brilliant that they look like flying silver dollars. We fly in unison and in harmony with each other like a flock of migratory birds. Every once in a while one of my wings brushes up against another bird and I can actually feel it against my body as we brush up against each other. The experience is so true to life.

I know at that moment I can choose never to return. All my senses known and unknown are fully alive. If I change course we all change course instantly. It is so exhilarating. Just to test it, I open my eyes and see my bedroom, which is dull in comparison. I want to be in flight so I quickly close my eyes again.

I feel I am an integral part of this new place and so fully alive that I do not want to leave. It is so true to life that I know if I never open my eyes again my awareness will never skip a beat. I will be part of this world and my old existence on earth I will soon forget.

I then suddenly have an idea to become a fish. With that thought, my little bird consciousness then descends at full speed down toward the waters upon the earth. I then hear a voice say, "Aren't you afraid, you are approaching the surface of the water?" I say, "NO, I'M NOT AFRAID! I WANT TO BE A FISH!" With that thought, I become a Neon Tetra fish swimming in a school of red and blue fish. I practice swimming among my school fish. I am responding to other fish requests and they are responding to me, never once losing step with the multitude of fish in the school. In front of us a different school of fish is approaching. We are on a collision course. I then hear a voice say, "Ruben, aren't you afraid of colliding with the oncoming school of fish?" I say, "NO, I'M NOT AFRAID!"

We swim with great speed between the waters of the oncoming school of fish and never do any members of either school collide. I then turn and look back and it hits me. I can breathe under water. The scene is so surreal I wonder if I have permanently left behind my former life on earth. I take another minute to breathe in the awesomeness of this new collective consciousness before I return.

I opened my eyes and found myself snuggled under my sheets with my two dogs, thinking how wonderful it is to be in the mind of God. It puzzled me why I was referred to as Michael. I learned that the name Michael means likened unto God and the Archangel Michael was said to be God's messenger. I can only surmise that the bearded man knocking at the door was Christ. Revelation 3:29 says, "*Here I am! I stand at the door and knock. If anyone hears my voice and opens the door, I will come in and eat with him, and he with me.*" I knew God had a message he was delivering to humanity through me and it had to do with answering the door. That door is found within the dream space. Anyone can have divine visions. It simply requires that you harness the dream space and overlay it onto your waking life. This is where the second coming of Christ takes place. The world within you is just as real as the physical world we experience in our daily lives. Our physical reality is actually a result of the collective dream. To bring Heaven to Earth we must become aware of what lies within and allow heaven to guide our lives. To live the dream is to have Heaven on Earth.

Another interesting point here is that the angels outside my windows had veils over there faces like mosquito nets. They could not see me until I called out to them. I realized I must ask for help in order to get help from the angelic realms. We ask for help through prayer and meditation. I also understood that the veils protect the angels from being misguided by the illusions we have created out of our fears. They in essence only see the good in us.

Having released my fears, I was then able to exchange my fear based veil with a new veil represented by the white sheer curtain through which I now see the earth. Today I have a choice; I can see life through a veil of fear or through a veil of unconditional love. It is the veil of unconditional love that creates for us Heaven on Earth and allows us to experience oneness with the rest of creation. We become connected to the Universal Mind, the governing and harmonizing force of the universe. We learn to communicate with this force and we see how it responds to the desires of the heart and we understand the Law of Attraction and the Law of Karma.

J. C. Penney Is Hiring, Inquire Within

When I woke up the next morning, I recalled a dream, which at first appeared to be too scatter-brained to possibly hold anything meaningful or profound. I was thinking, "Where's my burning bush?" I felt I had been doing all the necessary footwork and should at least get something more than a J.C. Penney dream. In the infinite wisdom of the universe this dream did in fact turn out to be my burning bush and my calling.

In this dream I am working as a floor salesman at J.C. Penney in the menswear department selling men's ties. (I have never worked in a department store in my life.) Christmas is approaching and I am thinking it would be nice to use my discount and give Joe

IN THE COURSE OF A DREAM EMANUEL FOR LOVE

a Christmas tie to wear at the Christmas party. The store is busy with holiday shoppers. I am at home getting ready to go to work and I look around the house to take an inventory of what I need to do to prepare the house for the upcoming holiday party. I can see that the stairs going up to the second level are crumbling from neglect and the light at the top of the stairs is turned off. I am only able to see halfway up the flight of stairs leading to the upper level of the house.

My mother has arrived early and wants to see all the improvements to the house of which I have been boasting. In particular, she wants to see the upper level of the house. In my haste to remodel the upper level I neglected the steps between the two floors. The fact is that my neglect of the steps has made my home not quite presentable. I tell her to go on up but to just be careful and watch her step. I am not sure what condition she will find the upstairs in. I do not have time to escort her through the house myself because I am eager to start my new job working for J.C. Penney.

I get to J.C. Penney and am walking through the different departments as if I were a shopper and not an employee. The other sales people are looking at me, thinking, "Why aren't you attending your department?" My friends, Luis and Liz, show up looking for a gown for Liz to wear to the party. I go over to help them shop and one of the sales people assigned to ladies fashions gives me a look as if to say, "Get out of my department." I am thinking, "Can't she see I'm an employee of J.C. Penney? Let her go work my department while I help my friends shop for an outfit."

Liz picks out a metallic baby blue dress that goes over one shoulder and down across her chest in an upside down V shape exposing her other shoulder. The dress is laced with tinsel along the edges.

There are three sisters (triplets) who are shopping for matching party dresses. The dresses they are looking to buy have exaggerated collars that are puffed up and showy. The dresses are a dirty Christmas red. I think to myself, "Look how childish they are to want to come as matching triplets; can't they express their own individuality?"

THE CALLING

I finally get back to my department and most of my ties have been sold. The only thing left are the real expensive silk ties like the ones Joe shops for. The remaining ties are priced at $358 each. There is only one silk Christmas tie left that is priced at $352. It seems like a lot of money to spend on Joe for a single Christmas tie that he will only wear once.

This dream has meaning at many different levels, some of which are highly personal. In this simple dream there is an epiphany--a spiritual awakening about to happen--which I would have overlooked had I gone with my initial wisdom and inclination to discredit the dream as the product of a scatter-brain--which is what most of us do every day. God's message comes in the still small voice of night. He does not make grand entrances, showing up at his party as triplets wearing pompous collars. I had to examine myself and ask the question, "How much do I value my spiritual connection, my *tie* to God?"

What this dream did was to help me sift through the ties and make a decision on which ones to keep. God was trying to point out where in my life I should draw my focus and work my steps.

The pathway between the lower self and Higher Self involves leaving behind those ties that bind us to the physical plane and the ego. We need to take inventory of our ties and get rid of those that are of lesser value, those that are not purposeful, and those that are not formed out of love. Ultimately we are faced with a choice between ties that dress up the ego in a party dress to look good for one night and ironically, on the other hand, one single tie that connects us to God and is good for all of eternity. Even for those who have found God, or Christ as you know Him, it is not about coming to the party looking like triplets with pumped up collars speaking in identical tongues. We need only come to the party wearing that one important Christmas tie regardless of the current state of affairs in which we find ourselves, as was symbolized by my home in the dream.

I found it interesting that the name of the department store was JC Penney. I understood the penny symbol because it emphasizes what I know to be God's way of reinforcing my path. It lets me know through the miracle of synchronicity that I am on the right path, which ultimately leads to a spiritual awakening. God places in my path a penny at the right place and at precisely the right time in groups of ones or threes. They have become my magic numbers to let me know without a shadow of a doubt that "God IS with me".

I then thought, "What could the J.C. stand for? Might it also have some hidden meaning?" At first, I could not think of anything. I wondered if J.C. were the initials of the founder of the store chain Penneys. And then it hit me: "The Founder of Pennies". "J.C." = "JESUS CHRIST". Jesus Christ is the founder of Pennies. He is the founder and I (we) are the finders. I have found CHRIST IN ME.

I nearly dropped dead. Though I might not have been the best floor salesman at J.C. Penney and my home may not have been perfectly presentable, I found a process through inquiring within the dream space, and faith in the synchronicity of the penny, that for me brought about a profound spiritual awakening.

Appointed Foreman of the Aquarian Age

> *"A man will meet you carrying an earthen pitcher of water; follow him into the house where he goes in."* (Luke 22:10; Mark 14:13)

The Calling

"And then the man who bears the pitcher will walk across an arc of heaven. The sign and signet of the Son of man stands forth in the eastern sky. The wise will then lift up their heads and know that the redemption of the earth is near." (The Aquarian Gospel 157.29,30)

I have been named Foreman.

I began my meditation by focusing and holding my attention on my third eye. It was like balancing on one foot. I felt like a figure skater gracefully navigating the waters of life. I was enjoying the ride and lost myself in the experience. I then saw from the calves down, the robe and sandals of a man. The man turned and walked along a path. I immediately issued the instruction to my consciousness to follow him and with that thought, my consciousness followed the man. I once again lost myself in the experience. My attention was suddenly refocused on a bright light that shown though a door frame. I suddenly found myself in a Buddhist or Hindu temple. I walked along its corridors marveling at the ornate design.

Again, I lost myself in the experience. I saw a man of authority issuing assignments to his people and he came to the assignment of Foreman and he looked at me and said the job of Foreman goes to Ruben. I was surprised as I did not think anyone knew I was there. I thought my consciousness was there simply observing, but suddenly the meditation became interactive, and I was being called to active duty. I saw the face of the man issuing the work assignments. His voice was familiar to me but I could not place him. The image then faded and I came out of my meditation. I thought I had better look up the exact definition of the word Foreman. I proceeded to look it up in Webster's dictionary.

Foreman:

Function: *noun*

: a first or chief person: as **a** : a member of a jury who acts as chairman and spokesman **b** (1) : a chief and often specially trained worker who works with and commonly leads a gang or crew (2) : a person in charge of a group of workers, a particular operation, or a section of a plant.

I have never been in any job capacity that uses the term Foreman. The term is not used in my day to day vocabulary, so this had to have come from some intelligence outside of me. I know I have stood at Heaven's Gate and offered myself to God that He may use me as an instrument of His will. To know that my petition to serve had been accepted has to be the highest honor that could be bestowed upon me. I gladly accept the right to serve as Foreman in service to the One.

There is a sense of knowing that is so strong in me it often makes me feel very uneasy. I ask myself, "Can I live up to the calling? Will anyone believe me? Will I inspire anyone to follow their dreams?"

I have never been one to want to be up front and center stage on anything. I am very much an introverted person. I cannot, however, let down those who are depending on me to carry out my purpose. What I have realized is that I am not alone. I am part of a collective. I work alongside many of those who are not in the physical realm. Because of this awareness, I must take the example and walk as if I am called to be the "man to carry the earthen pitcher and lead the people." Ironically, I was born under the sign of Aquarius, which gives the scripture special meaning for me. I must walk as if the message I have to share about dreams will lead millions down their inward path of illumination. The best thing about it is that I am not asking you to follow me. I am asking you to follow your own religion. I am asking you to follow your dreams.

The Force Is With You

> I am having a dream where I find myself in the attic of a very large old house. I do not like being here because it is a frightening place, but I know there is something here that I must confront. In the rafters, I see a creature wearing a dingy green hooded cloak. It sees me and begins to descend upon me. I am in utter fear but I know I have to confront it. I remember my therapist telling me once that if I was ever confronted by a scary creature in my dream to hold out my hand and introduce myself. Thinking this is just not the place for introductions, and acting against every fiber in my being, I hold out my hand and duck my head. From the corner of my eye I can see the creature's bony hand reaching out to meet mine. It grabs hold of my hand and I think to myself, "You've just sold your soul to the devil." All I can think is to pray, but for the life of me I cannot remember any words to any prayer. The only words that come to mind are, "Full of Grace, Full of Grace," which I repeat over and over. The creature then lifts its head to make eye contact with me and from beneath his hood I see his face. He is Yoda or a creature that looks just like Yoda from Star Wars. He looks at me and says, "The force is with you."

The only thing standing between us and God, the universe and the universal force of love within us is fear. Dreams provide us a safe place in which to confront all fears and in the process remove the veil that separates us from God. This allows us to see things for what they really are. To experience heaven we must first rid ourselves of all fears. Dreams are our salvation.

Jesus was right when he said, "I am the way, the truth, and the life: no man cometh unto the Father, but by me."

In the dream space there are a host of other fears not born of this world that we must also face. Once free from fear, the veil is removed and we can experience the light and walk through the Christ door that we must pass on our path to enlightenment or Christ Consciousness. It is not a choice, it is our destiny. As seeds we must sprout and grow to our full human potential. It is part of the human evolutionary process in which spirit is the guiding force.

Your Project Is Funded For Daisy

Last night, I was meditating and I lost myself in the experience. I saw a door so I immediately gave my mental self instruction to go through the door. The door opened up and I walked in. Hiding behind that door was Yoda, from Star Wars, without his green cloak. He welcomed me into his world. I was now in a hallway or passageway with a series of identical doors. Slowly each door opened up and behind each door was a person. Each person was different in appearance yet the doors they each stood beside were identical. It was like being in a men's locker room with shower stalls lining both sides and every person peeking around their individual shower door. We were all talking as we peeked around our doors. They were telling me that the research project I had proposed had been approved and funded for Daisy.

It was time for me to go but I did not want to leave because I was so curious about my surroundings; however, they all insisted it was time for me to get back. I knew the vision was coming to an end so I tried to retain as much detail as possible. I then found myself back in my bed. When I opened my eyes I could still see Yoda in the center of my room, and all the many faces lining the doors as each took his turn in saying goodbye. As they each closed their doors, the last one remaining was Yoda. He gave me a look that said, "I believe in you," then he quietly disappeared into a bright light as he closed my door.

I found it interesting that they used the word Daisy. I immediately asked myself, why Daisy? The last time I could remember having referred to the word daisy was in describing the concentric circles of arched angels as they absorbed the Light of Christ like daisies in the sun. According to my personal symbols, the daisy as a symbol refers to the way in which we absorb the Light of Christ, which for me comes through the process of harnessing the dream space and learning the meaning of my personal and trans-personal meta-symbols.

When experiences like this happen I come away with a profound sense of inner knowing. I know, beyond a shadow of a doubt, that I am in line with the Universal Force that is God and there is nothing I cannot do or achieve if done in the name of Love and for the greater good of man and myself.

Each time we give in this way we receive by the same measure tenfold. In this way there is always abundance.

Destiny's Child

"Don't you remember the day when you went away and left me?" I woke up this morning with the words to that song playing in my head. It is not a song I have in my library, yet I was struck by the clarity with which I was hearing the words. I then closed my eyes to do my morning meditation. As soon as I closed my eyes, I saw a man sitting in front of me who was apparently in the middle of a discussion with me. I had apparently been in his company the entire night. The man looked just like Jesus Christ. His facial features were perfectly formed in two tones, blue and grey. His image slowly faded as memory of the dream I had earlier that night came rushing back.

I am in a mansion with my partner who is off socializing and paying me no attention. It does not even feel like we have come to the mansion together because he has hardly spent any time with me. At the end of the evening, as the sun is coming up, I realize it is time for me to go and move on with my life, so I look for a place to take a shower in one of the many rooms of the mansion. I do not remember where I placed my key but I decide it is not important because I will not need it any more. After taking my shower I get dressed and proceed to leave. Those three black female singers, Destiny's Child, are staying at the mansion. I am honored that Destiny's Child is staying at the mansion the same night that I am there. Joe is still all wrapped up with himself and he does not even realize what is about to happen. As I leave, I tell Joe that I am leaving him. He still does not get it and he jokingly and antagonistically says he is going to head to a sex club and let it rip. I call him back and tell him that I do not want to ever see him again; I am leaving him for good. I walk out the front door with my motorcycle helmet under my arm. I feel like I am walking against a very strong wind but I am somehow able to keep going. As I am walking down the streets of the city, I pass a lonely bar at the edge of town where people are washing their clothes. I walk in and observe everyone busy washing their clothes. There is an aquarium in the very dark recesses of the bar. It is a really large aquarium with lots of beautiful silver fish in it. I know I have to get going but I cannot take my eyes off the aquarium and the fish in it. I am captivated by their beauty. I am walking away with my eyes still fixed on the aquarium, not watching where I am going and I accidentally bump into a bearded man. I excuse myself for not watching where I was going. He then asks if I would like to sit with him to admire the beautiful fish.

The Calling

We are Destiny's Child, trying to bring to our remembrance the day we left our inner sanctuary at the mansion with Christ. Dreams are a place where we can cleanse ourselves and find the strength to make those tough decisions that bring our focus and lives back to the silver fish, or angelic school of thought, our only true birthright.

Dreams hold Universal Truths. They are multi-dimensional and are perfectly formed with divine precision. They are the most precious spiritual gift we have at our disposal. From my experience, I have learned that all interpretations of dreams, assuming they "fit like a glove", are true and there is no single way of interpretation. Dreams can and often do have multiple valid interpretations. I believe sharing your dreams with others to gain additional perspectives is very helpful. The truth fits like a glove and you will know it when the fit is right. Once you have an interpretation or a couple of interpretations that fit like a glove, meditate on the symbols and the relationship between the symbols and you will find that the universe has a way through synchronicity of validating your interpretations to let you know you are on the right path. Spirit loves to tickle you in this way. It does however require that we remain aware because the work of spirit is always subtle. That is how we will know it is from spirit. It brings joy to our spirit guides that they have successfully assisted us in discovering our own truth about who we are.

For me, I have always found pennies in either single instances or groups of three, at precisely the right place and at the right time. You will find that your ability to recognize patterns and relationships to things and circumstances will greatly increase.

Everything in our world tells a story. There is nothing out of place. We are simply often not aware that a story is being told. It feeds our soul as we become appreciative of the greater picture and we realize that we are all interconnected. It is impossible to separate ourselves from the whole. It is so important that we share our dreams with our children and family and extend the fabric of the collective unconscious into our third dimension. This will bring Heaven to earth.

Fear - The Battle Within

The Mirrow People

The Mirrow People haunted me in dreams before and immediately after my near death experience, at a time when I really did not know what was happening to me. These were recurring nightmares. The Mirrow People were aliens who invaded the Earth and had a way of assimilating humans, taking on a person's features and identities and becoming the evil twin. I appeared to be the only person on Earth aware of their presence. They were cloaked and would invade and attack unseen. After assimilating a human, they would take on the human identity and blend back into society unnoticed.

I had some kind of natural ability to disarm them by focusing my thoughts on love. I would blink my eyes and with loving intent send wave after wave of thought out into the universe. They did, however, outnumber me and since I could not be in all places at once, I had to find a way of communicating what was happening to others in order to save the Earth.

It was difficult for me to distinguish the Mirrow People once they took on a person's identity unless I carefully observed their behavior and looked for patterns. At times, I was able to distinguish them by looking deep into their eyes, but fear kept me at a distance. I was a prisoner of fear. I was afraid of everyone. What good did my natural gifts do to serve me and allow me to survive their attack if I were to lose the human race to the hands of the Mirrow People?

The Mirrow People were aware and perplexed by my gift and they viewed me as a threat. The more I interfered with their mission by disarming them, the more they hurt me by assimilating people I love. I decided the only way to win was to teach the Mirrow People about Love and in essence assimilate them, but it was proving to be a very difficult task.

At the time the Mirrow People first appeared in my dreams, I was journaling with pen and paper. For some reason, every time I wrote Mirror People the word came out Mirrow. Once I started using a voice recorder and transcribing my dreams, my brain always seemed to transpose the 'r' for a 'w' every time, no matter how hard or how slowly I tried. Since the 'm' and 'w' are mirror opposites it seemed a natural mutation and it fit who they were. They were a mirror image initially representing the unknown shadow self. They were, however, mutable and later these fear-based character defects, when confronted and faced, became the foundation for spiritual principles. The Mirrow People helped me confront my fear of the unknown and the dark side within, which was exactly what I needed to enable me to receive the freedom of spirit and the new awareness I now have.

The Mirrow People vs. Humanity

Someone in my family purchased a house up on a hilltop in the suburbs of town. There are big mansions built of stone up in that area which remind me of what I imagine the homes to look like in the Austrian mountains. Their house is on the down slope of the side of the street, which places their front windows at ground level.

They are preparing to host a big dinner. They have prepared huge platters of food. I am not sure who is coming to this party. I am only close to one or two distant relatives here. They have remodeled the living room to make it bigger to accommodate all the guests. They have chosen a pale green and gold color theme for this room. It must be around 5 pm and half

Fear – The Battle Within

the food is already gone. They tell me the neighbors up the street are also having a party and they instruct us to take the leftovers up to them. I can sense there are Mirrow People all over the place. I am uneasy as I do not know what their intentions are. This family is not that generous to readily give up their leftovers. There must be some other motive.

I decide this is a good opportunity to see how these Mirrow People transform. I sense that they are definitely here, as though preparing for a major attack. We deliver the leftovers to the neighbors and I begin sensing extreme uneasiness. I hear screaming in the distance. It is almost as though they feed off these people, fattening them up with their leftovers. Something is calling on me to do something, but what is it that I am supposed to do? I have got to wander over to the neighbor's house at the top of the hill to see what is going on. I wander up the street dragging my cousin along with me. He has no clue what I am sensing or why the urgency of the matter. The sense of urgency is like the War of the Worlds; Mirrow People vs. Humanity. We need to get the secrets of their transformation. The problem is that we cannot tell who is who. In essence, this is a war of body doubles, good vs. evil, but who is who? The secret is at the top of the hill and I have to find it.

We look around the neighbor's house trying to avoid being swallowed up by these Mirrow People. They are eating and devouring everyone. This is where the screaming is coming from. There is some sex act on the TV -- some guy having oral sex. One of the girls at the party thinks we are members of their party and so we just go along with things to get more information on the nature of what is going on. I trick this girl into activating her transformation. She has a bottle or glass flask with a clear liquid in it. I get her to believe it is time to transform and to go tell the others. She eagerly agrees and drops the flask on the ground and runs off to tell the others. The liquid in the flask produces vapors and suddenly, there is a dense fog that engulfs the hillside. I can see the Mirrow People materializing before my eyes. They have ropes tied around their waists with the other end connected to their doubles in the physical world. They apparently have all their dirty work done by the body doubles who are enslaved to them. We have to break free and find the antidote that is located somewhere at the top of the hill.

In the Course of a Dream Emanuel for Love

We move quickly so that the vapors do not activate the Mirrow People. At the top of the hill we find a small blue velvet sack filled with foreign coins. Each coin has a head on it, apparently the image of someone. The coins look Canadian. Along with the head, the coins are numbered. I look at the coins to determine if there is a pattern I can quickly identify. I sense there is a riddle to be found in the coins that holds the secret to the transformation of the Mirrow People. It is too much information for me to process at once. I feel overloaded. I make it a point to commit to memory the three numbered coins: *(1), (2), (2)*.

I have to hurry. The Mirrow People are right on my heels, so we need to move and move fast. We make our way down the hill, hiding behind bushes to avoid being seen. My cousin picks up some food off one of the platters on the way down and is now too busy stuffing his face. He is no longer paying attention to me and the urgency of our mission. That is going to cost him his life if he is not quick to follow me. There are now people on horseback that appear out of nowhere. They seem to be policemen with rifles here to help defend against the Mirrow People. They give us a secret. The Mirrow People are apparently unable to swallow up salty people. I think to myself, we are all by nature salty people. How could that clue be of any help? I know my teardrops are salty. Maybe if we remain true to our nature we are guaranteed to be safe. We can consider that a Universal Truth. We must be in harmony with nature to be safe.

There are large, tall women warriors who are part of the Cavalry, who are able to defeat the Mirrow People by wringing their necks like chickens. It is almost as though there is good and bad within the Mirrow People and they too are fighting a civil war within themselves.

We have to move to a safe place where we can have time to ponder and process the riddle. My cousin is still procrastinating and I do not want to leave him behind but we need to move for our own safety.

Every dream holds a riddle to be solved that answers the question, "What am I supposed to do to set myself free and be all that I was meant to be?" The secret is stored at the top of the hill in the mind of man in whose shadow fear is cast in stone. We have built a house in which fear can dwell in our mind and we have given it liberty to expand its claim on the property we hold through our own self indulgence and greed.

By stepping into the observer role and listening to our inner voice we can trick our minds to see what really makes us tick. In the end we find that the only way to win is to focus our thoughts on love, teach love to others and allow ourselves to be transformed by it.

Why is it that we do the things we do? How do we take corrective action to change our behavior and align ourselves with love? There is that unseen Cavalry, our Higher Self, and spirit guides who are ever present in our time of need, to help us decipher the riddle found in the velvet blue sack at the top of the hill. We can be assured that by remaining true to our nature, we have nothing to fear.

Mutation of the Mirrow People

I am at a Halloween party looking for someone who might be able to help me set up my aquarium. I am afraid of social situations so I just want to find someone whom I can trust to help me and then get out of here. The person who lives here has several aquariums that are stacked one on top of another. I can see that they have red tail sharks, tin foil barbs and silver dollar barbs.

I am watching the fins on the fish. I do not know where the fish came from because they were not in the tanks when I walked in. Everyone has very good disguises, such that I cannot tell what parts of them are disguises and what is real.

There is a guy who walks in from the courtyard. Something about this guy makes me feel uncomfortable. I am sensing that I should not trust him. He does not stay long and soon after walking in proceeds to leave. I notice there is something different about him as he is leaving - something that was not there when he walked in. I look at him carefully, thinking that he may be a thief who has probably walked off with something that was not his and not part of his costume when he walked in. I notice he has a bloody hand on his shoulder. I am thinking he sliced someone's hand off and is wearing it as a trophy. That is not normal. I can see his other two hands so I know the hand on his shoulder is not his. I also notice that he has two miniature people on his shoulders. One is me and the other is the guy standing next to me. I walk over to the guy next to me to tell him about the miniature people. The guy walks off and does not seem concerned. I tell the guy that he should worry because the thief has a mini-me and a mini-him on his shoulders. I look out the door and the guy with the mini-people is headed for the gates to exit the property. I can see the mini-me. It looks like a monkey on his back and it is jumping up and down. I get the feeling that these mini-people might possibly be another group of Mirrow People that have come back in a slightly mutated form. Are we not able to recognize them? I now begin to hear the screams of people and I know my intuition is correct. There are Mirrow People present in disguises and with it being a Halloween party it makes their attack easier to conceal. It is a sneaky attack by a mutated form to catch us off guard.

    I am now in the last known refuge. The Mirrow People cunningly steal your identity, parade as you and assimilate you. You can tell them apart by carefully looking at their eyes head on. If you look at them at just the right angle you can see the laser light in their eyes. This particular mutation of Mirrow People has red pupils in their eyes. I remember the last incarnation before this one had blue laser light in their eyes. I do not know what the colors mean.

    They are now taking over the Cavalry because they were caught off guard. I am sensing a distress call. There seem to be some people among our allies that are able to go undetected by the Mirrow People. We have to be careful because we do not know what it is yet

Fear – The Battle Within

that causes them to be unable to detect us. It is almost as though they do not even see us. I might be one of the ones they cannot perceive because I am apparently still alive. We have been able to barricade ourselves in the upper part of the house. It is apparent that the Mirrow People believe they have consumed everyone but I know that they have not. There seems to be absolutely no communication among those they have not consumed, for fear that any communication might be detected. We are in essence frozen among them.

We do know one thing...this is the war of the worlds. It is confirmed that their intention is to consume and destroy us. We are among a group that by luck or grace have been spared. Otherwise, our world would be in complete annihilation. From our safe haven, I can see through the sky lights in the ceiling. I can see their space ships that fly overhead. It always puts fear in us because we never know if our cover has been blown. I can only imagine this is the way Ann Frank felt.

We constantly try to remain out of sight. I am gazing out at the sky and I see a space ship coming our way. They are headed for a train that is racing along the track loaded with people. Those on the train may belong to another isolated group that is trying to escape. The train operator quickly realizes that he cannot evade the space ship and attempts to jump the track. The space ship fires a laser at the train and blows up one of the cars. The train screeches to a halt.

We are worried about our safe haven. We have a data port and phone line that is connected. I am not sure if anyone has tried to use it. I sense that someone has and possibly managed to encrypt messages for help, but I do not believe I can decipher them. To survive we have to stay a few steps ahead of the Mirrow People. I think I have to get the key or pattern to use in our favor before the next mutation.

The Mirrow People have now taken on the properties of the men on horseback by consuming them. I see these beasts that have human heads on the bodies of horses, which

In the Course of a Dream Emanuel for Love

reminds me of some of the images from Greek Mythology. They are laid dead in the streets consumed by the Mirrow People. I am thinking I can hide behind or under a dead head on horseback but that would only work for a little while because the decay of the carcasses would soon be a problem. Around the side from where I am, I can see where the train crashed. It now serves as a separation for the two opposing camps. The dividing line now seems to be the railroad track. This is a dead zone. I can see the camp with my people as I knew them to be. They are jumping up and down yelling, but I cannot tell what they are saying. I think they are telling me to make a run for it and climb over the fence. Barbed wire lines the top of the fence.

  I can now see the red laser lights headed my way and I know that can only mean the Mirrow People are back. I think they sense someone is still alive on their side of the tracks. It is now or never. I start my run for it. My people open the fence slightly to let me in. I make it in but one or two Mirrow People also make their way in. We run up the mountain side to another hilltop where there is another home that is a safe haven. There is a sense of tranquility here. I see my people are now riding motorcycles instead of horses. This may be more effective for them. The Mirrow People start to infiltrate our space so we have to move again. There is a data line here too, to use in case of an emergency. I do not have an IP address to communicate so I do not know how to set it up. I put my ear to the wall plate to see if I can hear or perceive anything. I am at a point where I have no choice but to try anything. I hear voices saying, "Transmit the code, transmit the code," but I do not know what code they are talking about. Suddenly it becomes too much. I am sensing too much information. I am overloaded. I see the Mirrow People coming toward me so I begin to run, knocking over the table, the phone and all that is on the table. I inadvertently disconnect the line. I am afraid I might have fouled it up again. The problem is that I am not in full awareness of all the information I need. It is not a strategic plan because I am not involved...

Fear – The Battle Within

So much of my life has been ruled by fear, which has a paralyzing effect, keeping me perpetually stuck in time. Fear is relentless. The greatest hurdle we must overcome, with the greatest reward for doing so, is fear. Fear is the one thing that will keep us from realizing our true human potential. We can be like the fish of Christ; living in an environment that is protected and sustains a healthy and fulfilled life based on spiritual principles.

The fish is seen as a symbol for Christ and Christians. We are moving out of the Age of Pisces, which was marked by the birth of Christ. We are moving into the Age of Aquarius, which calls us to be the Aquarian; the keeper of the fish. As keepers of fish we become aware of the environments or dimensions in which those fish are kept. We must create an environment in which the fish, or Christ within us, is allowed to thrive.

Our physical bodies are disguises we wear that hide our true spiritual essence. Fear comes in like a thief in the night and takes away our ability to listen to our inner voice. It removes the loving hand of God and the blood that was shed and we remain to suffer the loss.

We live our lives at only a fraction of our full potential. Freeing ourselves from fear allows us to operate in the present, which is the only moment in time that is eternal and the only moment into which we can bring Heaven to Earth. The needle is threaded in the now. The Cavalry of support we have is essentially dead to us unless we learn to use the communications port hidden in the dream space. We must learn to listen to our inner voice and the best tool for doing so is through meditation. Meditation helps us develop the ability to listen and dream work provides the key codes or dream keys with which we will come to know our true nature by unlocking the encrypted mysteries of life that are stored in the subconscious. Let those who have an ear hear. It is time to learn to listen.

The Things Dreams Are Made Of: The Mirrow People and the Secret Bulb

I am sharing my place with someone by the name of Ruben Rodriguez, which is my birth name. I am not sure if this guy has stolen my identity. I pretend I do not recognize the coincidence since I have changed my name to Ruben Bailey. I am not sure if the other Ruben knows that he has my real name.

There is a heavy-set guy with him. I think they are squatters in my apartment but I have not up to this point addressed this with them. I tell them that it is now time for them to leave. Ruben and his friend walk out the front door and I am about to be the last one to leave but the phone rings. I close the door to go answer the phone. The person on the other end of the line tells me he is looking for my ex. As he is talking to me, I look through the window and see the heavy-set guy sitting in the courtyard on a bench. I suspect he is waiting for me to leave so he can return to my apartment. I wonder if this phone call regarding my ex is originating from the heavy-set guy's cell phone. I observe him and Ruben and their possible interaction with each other. As I hang up the phone, I clearly sense the presence of my ex leaving the room. I decide to wait a few more seconds to see if my suspicion is correct. It is as though they are watching and timing my exit. After waiting a few minutes, I go to open the door to leave and as I suspected, they are standing outside my front door, both Ruben and his heavy-set buddy. The heavy-set guy asks if they can come back in. There is apparently some connection between them and the presence of my ex. The only way this is possible is if they are Mirrow People. The Mirrow People are manipulators of reality and master illusionists and they are in cahoots with my ex. I do not want them sharing my apartment because they are all extremely cunning and manipulative.

FEAR – THE BATTLE WITHIN

Now they are both back in my apartment. I notice there is a rolodex on the table that the phone is on. It is turned to an index card with my ex's phone number on it. I have not called my ex in a long time. Just then the floor begins to shift and the patterns on the walls begin to change. I am trying desperately to stay in the reality I know. I know the Mirrow People are responsible for shifting my reality. I feel as though they are filming a movie and we are the characters in the movie here to amuse or entertain them in some way and we do not even know it. Are they making money off us or exploiting us in some way?

For the first time, reality is shifting before my very eyes and I am witnessing the process. There are two guys side by side, each one standing like a soldier next to a tree. As reality shifts, both trees begin to retreat back into the earth and the facades of buildings begin to rise where the trees once stood yet the two guys are unmoved--only their surroundings change. There seems to be purpose for them standing there and a sense of neutrality between the men. I do not know if the Mirrow People realize that I am aware of their shifting reality. I am sure if they do not know they will soon find out and it will not be long before they take some action against me. I have to find out their secret. I have got to get as much information about them as I can to protect myself.

My entire surroundings begin to shift again. I am struggling to stay in the current reality. If the Mirrow People control my reality that means they will be able to change things before I get there. I feel as though I am on a moving walkway and am struggling to stand still in the same place in time. I suddenly see the key to their secret. It is a transparent irrigation bulb. The bulb seems to be protecting a smaller bulb within it or seed of some kind which has a liquid filled sac behind it. Unlike the irrigation bulbs I have seen before, this one, aside from being transparent on the outside, has a stubby spout for its mouth opening. The outer bulb protects the content of the inside bulb. The secret is in the fluid it contains. The bulb looks a little dirty on the outside as if it had been in someone's anus to conceal it the way drug smugglers conceal drugs.

IN THE COURSE OF A DREAM EMANUEL FOR LOVE

A guy goes to inject himself with the contents of the bulb. I pull it away from him and the liquid splatters all over me. I splatter some liquid on him as well so that he will be subject to the same effects as I am. I am not sure what this liquid does but we are about to find out. The liquid becomes a vibrant luminescent lime green. I think to myself "Ah Hah!!" As the words come out of my mouth, I notice there is some liquid splattered in my mouth. I walk over to a mirror and open my mouth and I can see very clearly a full color video screen clearer than any flat panel or high definition screen I have ever seen. There is a video playing on it. How did it get inside my mouth? It appears to be a portal to another world. The luminescent lime green acts as a background similar to the one a weatherman might use to stand in front of.

Dreams undeniably help us see ourselves through the eyes of the true observer. The people we see in our dreams are reflections of who we are inescapably by birth. Dreams help us see ourselves in others and realize our interconnectedness and unity. In truth, we are in more places than one. Our surroundings may change but who we are in spirit is eternal, timeless and unchanging. We are the center of our universe. Dreams give us a window through which to see our multi-dimensional selves where the process of creation takes place. We are the ultimate creators of our reality.

Ultimately we come to realize that we are the Mirrow People; the very thing we are afraid of. We are in essence afraid of our own shadow and the fear based illusions we create. We have so identified with the observed that we forget we are also the observer. All we need to do is come up one level and return to the driver's seat once again to change our reality. We have turned over control of our reality to the Mirrow People. We must regain control by stepping into our Higher Self where truth exists and send out into the universe a new set of instructions by simply changing our perception. The universe must respond in kind to our shift in perception. The best set of instructions we can possibly send involve Love, Peace, Joy and Happiness because those are the very things that will be reflected back to us. Who does not want those things in their lives?

Mirrow Man Meets Anel

This morning I woke up early, laid in bed quietly and began my morning meditation. I was able to relax enough to achieve viewing of the rainbow night lights. I noticed today I was able to see the color white as well. The swirling rainbow colors were delighting my visual senses. It was very beautiful. I then said to myself, "I want to go deeper and do some astral traveling this morning. Take me somewhere; anywhere." I then began to see a dense blue fog and in the foggy distance a thousand points of light like stars in an overcast sky. I then began to hear voices. They were clearly audible but the words they were saying for some reason did not register. I did not think much about it because I did not want to disturb the meditative state in which I was in. By this time, I was in such a deep trance that I could not move my body yet I was fully conscious. I was not seeing anything except the lights, yet apparently I had full audio going on. This was the first time I had experienced live audio in my head. There were voices I recognized from the past.

I must have entered a lucid dream state because all of the sudden I was at a party where they were offering me something to sniff. Not knowing what it was and without thinking, I sniffed it and it turned out to be ether. I thought, "OH NO!! I can't be sniffing ether. What are you doing? You have just compromised my sobriety." The ether, however, allowed me to hear other voices. I could hear them but I could not see who was speaking. I became paranoid and wanted to come back. I came back to the state where I could once again see the rainbow lights. I opened my eyes and looked around the room. I could move my body once again so I looked again to make sure everything was in its place. I confirmed I was awake.

Assured that I was not high and had not compromised my sobriety, I returned to my meditation and instantly I could hear the voices again. It sounded as though they were in the hallway or in my bathroom. Knowing no one was in the house with me but still slightly paranoid I tried to kick the closet door to let them know I was hearing them but my body once again would not respond. I could see the closet door in my room clearly, but no matter how hard I tried, my body just would not respond. I then saw a woman in spirit enter the room and stand between me and the closet door. She looked down at me. I did not recognize her but I could distinctly see her face. I instantly froze. I continued to watch her looking down at me. She quickly examined me and said I was okay and moved on. "Who was this woman?" I thought to myself.

I remembered from my meditation readings that there was nothing really to fear in any of this, so I tried to calm down even though I could not move my body. I meditated on the lights and tried to go back. Once again, I began hearing the voices coming from the hall or bathroom. I could clearly hear someone opening the bathroom drawer. Did they not know I was there? I tried with all my might to kick the closet door next to me, which was partially open, to make a noise so that they would know I was listening, but I could not move the closet door. I was getting frustrated. I had a feeling of being violated. I knew no one could possibly be in the house. The voices were clearly audible yet the words still did not register. Glued to the bed, I struggled to open my eyes and look at the closet doors. I opened my eyes and could clearly see them.

FEAR – THE BATTLE WITHIN

I once again meditated on the night lights. I could hear footsteps in the hallway and someone walking up and down the stairs. I thought, "This is not fair. I cannot do anything about the voices."

I then saw a video screen with a video playing on it. It was a video of the Mirrow People fighting an internal war within themselves. They had come here to fight an internal war against good and evil and I was caught up in the middle of it. On the video, I saw a group of Mirrow People enter what looked like my bedroom with firearms in hand. They begin firing their weapons in the direction of my bed. I could not see who they were firing at but from the video it looked like they were firing their arms at me. I cried out to God, telling Him I would never side with evil. I am a soldier for Him and I will die believing in God.

All I could hear was the firing of weapons. Their shotguns only incited more fear. I, on the other hand, remained unharmed. Empowered by their inability to harm me, I finally managed to get out of my body and into spirit. I pursued them into the hallway and down the stairs to the living room. The Mirrow People had retreated to the basement. With courage and fearlessness, I ran down the stairs and into the basement fully determined to put a stop to their infringement on my life. It felt like I was in a coal mine. It looked as though they had reached the end of the line. I saw one of them, with nowhere else to go, turn around in spirit and whiz right back toward me and past me. Instantly I give instructions to my consciousness to back up and pursue her. I could not let her get away. Now heading in reverse, my consciousness picked up speed and passed her up. I wanted to see her face. I had to see who this person was. As the person's face came into view, I recognized the person as

In the Course of a Dream Emanuel for Love

Anel. Instantly I stopped. I awoke and opened my eyes. Dear Lord, who was that?

How did I know that person as Anel? I did not even know who Anel was, but yet on some level I knew exactly who she was. I had to go back and find out what was going on and find out about Anel. Again I returned to my meditation. I recited the Lord's Prayer and told myself I wanted to astral travel. I slowly felt myself rise out of my body in spirit form. I began hearing a voice and noise again in the bathroom. Determined, I willed myself to go to the bathroom to confront whoever was there. I got up out of bed in spirit and walked down the hall to the restroom. The restroom light was off but I could tell there was someone hiding near the toilet. I yelled, "Get out of there." A blue apparition rushed by me and down the stairs. I went running after it. I could tell by the blue light trailing it that it had gone to the basement. I rushed down there, becoming more and more frightful all the time and reciting the Lord's Prayer in my head, but I was so nervous that I could not remember the words. The basement was pitch black. I paused halfway down the stairs and as I did the apparition peaked around the corner. It was the face of a radiant young girl in spirit form with a full head of beautiful golden hair. She looked at me with love in her eyes. I stood bewildered and amazed. I could not believe my eyes. What was I afraid of?

What was I afraid of? This out of body experience reinforced the lessons previously delivered by way of my dreams. I was the Mirrow Man in a struggle with myself.

The mistake we make is the belief that we are separate and autonomous. The illusions we create, such as fear, cannot possibly hurt us because we have created them. It is only when we believe in the illusions and accept as truth the idea that we are separate, that we feel the pain and discomfort of the separation that the illusions create. "Who is running from whom?" is the question I have to ask myself.

The first thing that struck me was the young girl's name. The instant I saw her face a part of me knew exactly who she was. Where had we met and how did I know her? Curiously, my spell checker did not recognize the name Anel as a proper name and suggested a correction of the name Anel to Angel. Could she have been an Angel who came to help me confront my fear? The woman who entered my room in spirit form, was she an Angel, too? Was the name Anel purposefully delivered as part of the riddle? So many unanswered questions remained, but as time and experience unfolded, a pattern began to emerge that left no doubt in my mind. It was an unshakable truth I would come to know for myself, one we would all realize sooner or later.

There is Nothing to Fear in Spooksville

I had a dream that Halloween was coming up. In the dream I am overhearing someone ask if they are planning to allow the ghosts to roam free in Spooksville and reopen the haunted house for visitors this year. Spooksville is a part of town people fear and avoid because rumor has it that there have been frequent ghostly sightings in the area and no one wants to be caught there alone. I am at a gas station filling up my tank of gas when I hear the gasoline attendant say that they are planning to open the haunted house in Spooksville early before Halloween and, as a matter of fact, tonight is the night.

I then realize that the gas station I have pulled into is actually within the Spooksville city limits. "Oh no," I think to myself. Here I am unknowingly in the wrong part of town alone. I have my dog Butters with me but he is a toy poodle and is of no protection. I sit my dog Butters in the baby chair of a shopping cart that was left at the gas station while I pump my gas and pay the attendant.

I am rushing to finish filling my tank so I can get the hell out of town when I notice the grocery cart is now rolling down the street. Now I have to leave my car unattended to run after the shopping cart because Butters is still sitting in the baby seat. I manage to grab him from the cart before it rolls into the street. I go back to finish pumping gas, then get into the car to drive off when I notice there is a traffic jam of cars backed up trying to get out of town. Cars are backed up for miles. We are told they decided to do some road work and dig a trench across the highway. They are not letting any traffic out of town. I feel trapped with no way out. I get out of my car and walk over where the road work is occurring and I can see the deep trench they have dug in the ground. It reminds me of the holes they dig to bury coffins. Looking at the cross section of earth I can see a very thin layer of asphalt followed by a very thick layer of Styrofoam followed by the brown earth below. As I look at the unusual layer of white Styrofoam I realize that the asphalt is an illusion. It is no more than a Halloween prop. It is Styrofoam painted black to create the illusion of real asphalt. It then occurs to me that this fear I am running from, which has been perpetuated by rumors, is merely an illusion. There is really nothing to fear in Spooksville.

The things we fear have no more basis than the Halloween props we stick in our yards to scare the children. We feed into rumors and follow the next person instead of looking below the surface of the ditches we dig ourselves into. There is nothing to fear in Spooksville.

At Home with the Aliens

As I slowly became more self-assured and less fearful, the Mirrow People morphed back into just plain aliens with no intensions on subverting my identity. What remained for me to face was the plain and simple fear of the unknown.

I had a dream that we were being invaded by aliens and that these aliens were trying to get me to open the window between our dimension and theirs. I have had many alien dreams in the past but this one was so real I felt it had actually come true. I had a false awakening where I thought I had woken up. I looked out the window to discover we were in fact being invaded by aliens. My suspicions were right all along. I could see an alien on the other side of my bedroom window motioning for me to open the window. I was thinking, "Oh my God, this is not a dream. It is real. We are in fact being invaded by aliens."

My fear and panic woke me up in real life. I opened my eyes and there beside my bed was a little creature. Of course, I now know these little aliens are nothing more than harmless faeries, pixies, elves and gnomes. They are Santa's little helpers or God's thought manifestations, however you care to view them, and they are with us all the time. The highest form of faeries is of course the angels and archangels.

The little guy was peaking over the side of my bed. I blurted out to him, "What are you doing scaring me like that?" He gave me a look as if to say, "What do you mean, I was just trying to get you to open the window so I could visit with you."

"I am asleep," I told him.

He then replied, "Okay, I'll just stay right here and watch over you tonight."

In the Course of a Dream Emanuel for Love

I then rolled over on my back, thinking, "Darn those aliens!" I decided to take advantage of this moment for some quiet meditation.

I quickly fell into a deep sleep where once again I was dreaming about being invaded by aliens. There were three groups: the good aliens, the bad aliens, and then of course us.

Our society is just now finding out about the aliens so they have the upper hand on us since they have the ability to remain cloaked hidden beyond our dimension and watch over us. In the dream, I am the only person who can actually see beyond their cloaking mechanism, so I am trying to help the good aliens get word to humanity about how the cloaking works so that we can disarm the alliances with evil and save the world. The problem is the obvious communication barrier. The good aliens speak a different language so I have to learn how to communicate with them first. I initially perceive all aliens to be a threat only because I do not know any better. I am beginning to see that there are good aliens wanting to help the world survive this evil threat. Of course, the bad aliens also know that I can see past their cloaking mechanism and disguises so they are out to get me. For some reason, they cannot directly hurt me but they can put obstacles in my way and make life difficult for me through illusion and manipulation. This is when I begin to realize that the good aliens are trying to protect me against the influences of the bad aliens. To remain safe, I must remain deep within the alliances with good.

The aliens are able to travel great distances using something similar to a slingshot that catapults them near where they want to go with simply a thought. They can catch up to us and overcome us very quickly, especially by using intimidation and fear. They also have the ability to materialize and blend in unnoticed like a cancer cell in remission. Once the transfiguration occurs, you cannot tell the aliens apart from the humans. You must witness the transfiguration to know that so and so is alien and not human. The trick to capturing them and arresting the evil ones is to catch them in the transformation process.

FEAR – THE BATTLE WITHIN

The good aliens are showing me that if you shoot them with a multi-colored paintball as they are transforming it will change their DNA structure and they will be forever tagged and the evil will be arrested. I then begin directing the paintballs at those I see transforming. The human police come right behind me and arrest those covered in paint. As the evil ones become aware of the hole made by the paintball in their cloaking mechanism they try to reverse the transformation process, which is apparently impossible and actually causes severe bodily deformities upon reconstitution. They have no choice--they cannot go back once struck by a paintball. At this point, I have to surrender to the process and help save the world. It is the right thing to do.

Even though I am already a good person at heart, I still have to pledge to be good. I do not want to be a crippled person so I have no choice. I understand the consequences of choosing the dark side. I pledge my allegiance to good and the war ends.

I then meet this guy with whom I fall in love. He is a Latino guy just like me who has great love for his parents. On this day, we are at his parent's house and he is doing all sorts of good deeds for them. Even though he is paying more attention to his parents, I know that come dinner time he will always pull up a chair and sit next to me. I also know that come bedtime we will hold each other tight all night long. It is the best relationship I have ever had. I am so in love with this guy and I truly believe and know that he loves me with all his heart, mind and soul and that he is committed to me and the pursuit of all that is good.

In the morning I woke up and upon opening my eyes, I saw a huge guy standing tall over my bed. He had vibrant orange hair, an orange beard and orange hair covering his entire body. He was massive, a gladiator of sorts. He was the little guy who peaked up over my sheets, except that from this vantage point he was larger than life. I saw him take the palm of his hand and run it along my body, gently pressing down into the sheets as a father tucks in a child.

In the Course of a Dream Emanuel for Love

When he touched me, I could feel his energy flow through my entire body. I was not afraid. I closed my eyes and fell back to sleep. A short time later, I woke up again because the dog began to bark. I opened my eyes and once again there standing on my bed was my orange gladiator watching over me. I thanked him and told him I would be right back. I went downstairs to let the dogs out. With this kind of protection watching over me, it made me want to just climb back into bed and curl up into a ball, which is exactly what I did upon returning from letting the dogs out.

I then had the following dream where I was given a map with which to find my way back home.

It is a geological survey of a plot of land showing the footprint upon which my house is built. I am looking at the map studying it carefully, not knowing north from south or east from west. The legends are writing in symbols; a language I am unfamiliar with. I am thinking, "How am I ever going to find my way back to this plot of land upon which my house is built?"

I begin turning the map, thinking maybe if I look at it from a different angle I might be able gather some insight on a possible direction to head in. The plots of land are clearly outlined and marked on the map with an 'X that marks the spot' where my house was built. Looking at the map, I am still clueless. How am I ever going to find this place?

A gentle wind blows and the map flies out of my hands and comes to rest upon the ground in front of my feet. I am suddenly awestruck. I realize that the plot of land upon which I am now standing is the exact same shape and size as the plot of land shown on the map. From this vantage point, I am able to clearly see both the map and the plot of land upon which I stand. I am home.

Fear – The Battle Within

As we learn about those things that are alien to us, the unseen and little known realms in which spirits exist, we must ask whether or not evil is real, and if it is, how does it influence and affect our lives? One thing is clear to me from this dream and from my experience. Evil does exist. We are endowed with a free will by which we can choose to live our lives in darkness feeding off the fear and illusions to which we subject ourselves and those around us.

Evil is a result of the belief and acceptance of the illusion that we are separate from God. Evil is held by those who believe that they can remain separate and autonomous. We buy into evil unknowingly through our belief in the illusions that fear and intimidation create. If, however, I accept that the lessons handed down to me in the name of love are correct and true, then I have already accepted that there is nothing to fear as long as I remain deep within the alliance of good.

We must remain deep in the alliance of good because we are of a weak mind and easily frightened. What I now must learn is how to respond to evil. What I have been taught by my spirit guides and consistently within my dreams, visions and experiences, is that evil cannot hurt you unless you accept it into your life and align yourself with it. Evil uses fear and intimidation to make you believe it has power over you but it does not unless you allow it to by buying into the fear it creates. Our birthright is to be one with God. Where there is light there is no darkness.

We do, however, have a responsibility to those lost in darkness because we are ONE. We must send them love filled thoughts; those multi-colored multi-dimensional paintballs to help paint a better picture and create a better world. The process of gathering our colored paintballs and arming ourselves begins within us. As we begin the process of awakening and are able to perceive the colored night lights, we also see in meditation our third eye looking back at us filled with the light of spirit, pulsating with the many colors of the rainbow, and as we begin our travels and become the pupil of that loving eye, we will understand the orbs through which we pass. We will string together the orbs like pearls on a string to form the silver cord and will understand the paintball effect. It is something that cannot be described but we know it when we see it.

We must awaken. To resist is to become handicapped within the human condition. The war ends when we surrender to the Universal Law that is governed by Love and align with it. To find ourselves and learn to love ourselves promises to be the best love we will ever experience. God and the Heavens really do watch over us. Dreams provide the map with which Spirit guides us home through a language born of symbols where few words are spoken. In the end we come full circle and realize we have never left our home. Heaven is where we make it. Dreams cannot help but inspire and produce a sense of awe.

Heaven's Warrior – Battle within the Dark City

This night I had a very somber dream.

I find myself in a very dark city. The streets are wet from rain and the clouds are dark and grey. The inhabitants of this city are being infected by a disease brought by aliens. People do not even know what is about to happen to them.

I have seen the progression of this extremely contagious disease. Everyone who comes in contact with it will come down with the symptoms. The disease is like Ebola, where the flesh boils. I can see the first few people suffering with the disease. I can smell the stench of their flesh. I try to run from the disease but people are actually still helping others, not

FEAR – THE BATTLE WITHIN

knowing that they are at risk. People's homes have been taken over by aliens. Communications are down so people in affected areas cannot warn others.

I manage to escape. People are finding homes in abandoned buildings and simply lying down to die. There is a stadium in the city. The bleachers are dark grey and all that is left of the seats are stumps. Some areas of the stadium floor have red markings. I am thinking that maybe the colors of the team that played there had red in them like a red arrow or red thunderbolt. For some reason, I am getting an intuitive feeling that if everyone just manages to make their way to the stadium that somehow their lives will be saved. They will then be able to live again.

I go around trying to spread the word to those close to the stadium but many have given up and those who have not are headed into harm's way. I then see someone in the military—a woman--coming at me with a machine gun. I close my eyes, bracing for the end, and saying to myself, "I wish they wouldn't play this scene out, I wish they wouldn't play this scene out, I wish they wouldn't play this scene out."

I opened my eyes, now awake in my bed and shaking my head. I then realized I was dreaming. As I looked around my bedroom, I could see the image of the military woman with her machine gun pointed at me standing at the foot of my bed. She had her machine gun pointed squarely at me. She then extended her hand out toward me with her palm up as though she had come to offer me assistance or rescue me and lift me up out of darkness. I was still fearful and unsure but I did not want to let her know that I was afraid so I remained motionless. She shot her gun at me, but instead of bullets coming out, balls of red light came out like paintballs. I could feel each pulsating ball hitting me and shaking me to my core. I could still see her hand extended toward me, palm up. I could see her lips moving as she talked to me but I could not hear her voice. However, I understood her to be telling me to grab ahold of her hand anytime I needed her and to trust and believe in what had been taught to me, for it is the truth and the truth is what will set you free.

From previous dreams, the symbol of the stadium for me has come to represent the head and skull and with it the mind and the third eye. The stadium opens up to the crown chakra above the head. Most of us are living in the dark city, lost and suffering from a diseased way of thinking that tells us we are separate. We have lost the means to communicate and receive divine guidance and assistance. We live in fear, too afraid to even recognize where our help may be coming from. If we could only make our way back to the stadium within the mind and re-establish communication through our crown chakra, we could save ourselves from the suffering in which we find ourselves.

I know my projection of fear will cause me to perceive my angelic help as military or as police officers with machine guns. Here, thankfully, I was the recipient of a red paintball, which I believe was intended to awaken the life force or Kundalini, that originates in the root chakra whose color is red. By awakening the life force and allowing it to flow though the chakras and up into the third eye and out through the crown chakra, we re-establish the vital communication link that allows us to receive the loving hand of support from our guardian angels.

Heaven is a place where very few words are spoken. Most messages from spirit that I have received have been sent telepathically, where I could see lips move but I could not hear any words being spoken. However, somehow I knew at a deeper level the message that was being delivered.

Next time, with courage, I will take that leap of faith and extend my hand out so that I may hold on to the loving hand of God's messenger.

Wrestling with Demons

Temptation of the Shadow Self

Before I go into this dream, I would like to elaborate a little on my reference to moonstruck images. I briefly mentioned them in an earlier dream. The visions have come to me in many different forms. Some are purely etheric within an illuminated fog of some kind while others are extremely exact two-dimensional shadows, blotches or geometric shapes. These are always solid black on a single colored or gradient colored backdrop such as shades of orange or blue. The images are so exact and precise it is clear they are not random abstractions. I suspect they hold some kind of symbolic code that might possibly serve to unlock parts of the mind or parts of our genetic code that lie dormant within our being. This is something scientists will want to study, but for now, I'll make reference to these types of two-dimensional visions as moonstruck images.

In this dream I am being mauled by groups of people wanting to have sex with me. I do not want to have anything to do with them. If I were going to have sex with someone why would I chose to do it in the open? Sex is a private thing that should be carried out in a private setting.

One of the members of this group then begins to try and court me like a pigeon, following me all around.

IN THE COURSE OF A DREAM EMANUEL FOR LOVE

I live on the inside of a secured housing complex on a mountainous hillside. All the homes in this community are white. The setting reminds me of Greece except that there is no water.

I am trying to avoid this pigeon person as he is pursuing me too aggressively. I do not want to associate with anyone who is so desperately looking for someone to be with. This person will apparently be with anyone who accepts his advances. This type of person could not possibly have anything meaningful to offer me.

Somehow he manages to gain entry into the secured perimeter of the housing complex. I am thinking, "Well, now that we are within a secure location maybe it is a sign that everything is okay. I do not have anyone in my life that I am seeing now since Joe, my ex, has left me; maybe I should give it a try and allow myself to meet someone."

By this time, I have walked to an area overlooking all the homes in the community. I can see all the white rooftops and their secluded yards. I have never been privileged before so now that I am up here, I am curious to know how these people live. Everything is so simple on this side. There are white houses with lush green lawns, a few tennis courts, and a lot of trees. This is what life is all about up here--very quiet and peaceful. I then look down and there is a black van entering the complex. I can hear its occupants arguing among themselves. This does not look good. They are going to disrupt the peace in the community. How did a black van get in here? This is supposed to be a peaceful housing community.

I then put two and two together and realize these people that entered the complex are somehow associated with this pigeon guy who has been following me. He cannot possibly have any good intentions. I am now thinking, "How do I get away from this guy? I made him believe I might be interested in him. The guy comes up wanting to have sex with me and I am trying to push him away."

During this struggle, I woke up in real life and opened my eyes. I could see the guy from my dream standing beside my bed with his pants down, tempting me and stroking himself. Immediately, I began saying prayers of protection for myself and said a blessing for him in the hope of freeing him from the dark side. Upon saying the prayer, he immediately vanished.

I then laid back down but had trouble falling asleep. I began seeing moonstruck images against a red orange and yellow backdrop. The images were of people engaging in acts of violence toward one another. Even though they were just moonstruck people, I could not stand to see them fight amongst themselves. I then saw a translucent red man. He was the only moonstruck image that was not solid black. He was glowing red with short stubby horns upon his head. He crawled in and among the moonstruck people, inciting violence and spurring more violence. He had to be the Devil himself. The Devil gave the moonstruck people rifles, which they used against one another. Every time a person was killed, that person would fall to the ground, be taken up by the earth, and instantly reappear behind the opposition force. It was clearly a vicious and unending circle without purpose.

I could not stand to see this violence among my people. They needed my help. If prayers helped me, prayers might help them. Once again I prayed for protection for myself. I visualized God's white light descending upon my house, upon the city, upon the country and upon the earth. I then blessed the moonstruck people including the Devil himself. I saw white and blue balls of light hailing down upon the red earth like meteor showers. The rage in the moonstruck people became subdued and the backdrop went from orange and red to a cool blue. The Devil was forced to retreat into darkness.

In the Course of a Dream EMANUEL FOR LOVE

    As peace returns among the moonstruck people, I fall into a dream in which I have a false awakening. I think the dogs are barking to go out, so I get up out of my dream bed and walk down the stairs to let the dogs out. As I am waiting for them to finish their business to let them back in, I notice water leaking from the ceiling adjacent to the kitchen where I am standing. I put my hand out and feel the droplets of water hit my hand. It is a leak. I grab a pan from beside the stove and place it on the floor. I make sure the drops of water are dripping into the pan. Looking at the ceiling above my head, I notice the water has made a white ring on the ceiling as if it dried and dripped for a long time. "How unusual," I think. "Why haven't I noticed the leak before and more importantly, where is it coming from?" Listening for clues, I then hear my roommate in the shower upstairs. I think maybe the white ring is a result of soap film and not an extended period of dripping. Having my doubts about the origins of this sudden leak, it occurs to me to look around and examine my surroundings. As I look around, I realize that I am dreaming. Besides, my roommate was not even home tonight. I then become fully lucid within my false awakening.

    With determination to see if this has anything to do with my tempter, I proceed to look around for more telltale signs. I walk down the hall and into my dark pitch-black living room. My vision becomes tunneled and I know I am going against the dream. I feel like I am a blue night light in a dark room looking through a blue halo. Everywhere I go, the room illuminates slightly. I know I am definitely going against the dream. I have to know more so I proceed and keep walking. My eye catches what appears to be a dark spirit standing in my living room off in the distance. It is a woman who is void of any light. I confront her, asking her what she is doing in my house. I bless her and begin reciting the Lord's Prayer. She freezes in place, not expecting me to walk in this dream. She seems more afraid of me than I am of her. As I approach her, I grab her firmly by the shoulders to escort her out the door. My hands touch her. I am shocked and amazed that I can actually feel the pressure of my touch against her shoulders.

The shock of feeling her presence instantly woke me up. I opened my eyes and there beside my bed was this woman. I could see the terror in her eyes. This woman had never experienced such a thing before. I suddenly knew she was an earth-bound spirit trapped within her own fear. I instantly felt compassion for her and began sending her love. With a look of total surprise, she fainted, her eyes rolling back, as her head fell. Her face then began to illuminate with the familiar blue light of spirit. Her body began to float up into the Heavens as she was released from darkness. Her illuminated spirit continued floating until I could no longer see her anymore. At that moment my alarm clock rang. Too late, I was already awake.

This was a powerful experience that demonstrated the hidden treasure of truth that lies just below the conscious mind, waiting for us to discover it. Without exception, this truth can be found within each and every person. If we allow our dreams to guide our lives, I know peace will come to all corners of the world. This message of Love must be carried by every light bearer to the ends of the earth. This is not about religion. This is about the God breath within the soul of mankind.

We live on the inside, where every home is pure and white, secured and protected. It is a place where peace and harmony is found. We are pure spirit having a human experience. Ironically, we are the moonstruck people. It is our choice whether to allow disharmony and negativity into our lives, but even that is only an experience. We must come to realize that to engage in evil against another is to do ourselves harm. The only proper response to evil is unconditional love and prayer. We must stop the violence. It is the only thing that will arrest the vicious circle and it begins with learning to love ourselves from the inside out. When we go inside ourselves we ask the questions, "How do those that love themselves live?" "What does this way of life look like?"

No, Neton, We Are Not Available

This night I started to see a dream vision where I was with Joe and we were walking out of some bar. As we exit the bar and turn to the left to walk down the narrow sidewalk, we see a group of thugs headed our way. They are not about to move or change their course to allow room for us to pass, so I walk to the right and Joe to the left to allow them to pass us. As I move to the right, one of the guys moves intentionally to block me. He is right up to my face trying to intimidate me. I am now worried about Joe because he is alone on the left side. I struggle to get around the guy.

The struggle jars me awake. As I open my eyes, I can still see the guy who was blocking me. He is right up on me giving me a threatening look so close I can literally feel the pressure and weight of his spirit on me even though I am awake.

It happened so quickly I was not sure if someone had actually broken into my house or if it was a spirit presence. I flung my arms at him to get him off me. I confirmed it was an evil spirit. I could not believe what had just happened to me. Who was he and why was he threatening me? Slightly scared and not knowing what to think, I curled up in a ball and returned to my sleep.

I then had a dream that Joe and I were standing at a bar. Two guys walk in who are known to us. One of them is someone who has always spelled trouble and who I dislike to no end. I cannot stand this guy. He comes over to poke his head into our conversation. With intention, I swing my left arm and hit the guy in the face hard with my watch. The guy is annoyed and bleeding from his eyes and nose. He does not know what happened but assumes unconvincingly that it must have been an accident. He does not know I intended on hitting him, but I did not expect to hit him that hard to cause him to bleed. I grab a napkin from the bar and offer it to him to wipe the blood off his face. He had come over to invite us to get together sometime. We respond hesitantly, "Oh sure." As he is about to walk away he says to me, "Oh, I forgot to mention, Neton says hi." I turn to Joe with a puzzled look, wondering who is Neton.

I threw this dream in here to show that not all dreams are pretty. Spirits can and do visit us in our dreams and that definitely includes Satan. As Christ was tempted, so we too must wrestle with our own demons. Evil moves with intention. Everyone has a dark side that they must confront and stand firm against, and to which they must say, "No." Satan does not want to lose those parts of us that might have been formerly aligned with evil or that have believed in the illusion of fear. Satan feeds off the energy we expend on fear. It is cash in his pocket. The only way to survive in darkness is to feed off the light expended by those who believe in the separation and fear-based illusions. As we awaken and become conscious of how we use our energy, evil will slowly dissipate. For this to happen, we must embrace our oneness and focus our thoughts on Love.

I have been shown time and time again that Satan can intimidate us, but he cannot touch us. As long as we do not invite him in, there is nothing to fear. We need not even flinch.

We Hold the Skeleton Key with which to Open the Door

I woke up in the middle of the night when I felt a very sharp pinch on my hand. I looked at my hand and I could see green angel hair all over it. I felt where I had been pinched and I could clearly see the fiber like strands of angel hair still vibrating with the light of spirit. I squeezed the hair between my thumb and forefinger in awe of its beauty. I looked over to my left, toward my closet doors, and saw a luminescent green hand coming out from around my closet door. The hand held a rather large ornate skeleton key which measured about 1 ½ inches in diameter, with a fancy 3 half-circle end on it. The hand was trying to use this huge key to open the door. I understood the message to be this: We hold the key in our bodies. Our Higher Self holds the door. Together our three circles are complete and in this way we open the door to our Christ Consciousness.

Why Do You Avoid Me? – The Addict That Just Will Not Die

I am dreaming there is a guy who is addicted and for some reason is showing up everywhere I go. I cannot for the life of me escape or run from him. He always seems to find and track me down no matter what I do or where I go. He is always there. He ran out of drugs a long time ago but has somehow found a way to get high naturally on the chemical residue left behind from all the years in which he has used. His body, I guess, has remained toxic even though he has not taken any more drugs.

This guy turns up everywhere I go. No matter where I am, there he is. I want to get away from him because I do not want to get caught up in his chaos nor his lifestyle. I finally distract him long enough and somehow manage to free myself of him by hiding on a book shelf. Before I know it he has found me again. I want to get high just to escape from him, but he is selfish and will not share his natural high with me. He will not let me be and he will not share.

WRESTLING WITH DEMONS

We are building this wooden deck that overlooks the woods and the trees in the back of the house. I find out the wood used to build this deck is from outer space and has alien termites that are eating it away from the inside out. I know that eventually the deck will not be able to sustain the weight of anyone standing on it.

Grace is with me and we are talking to a friend of hers from her childhood who is selling her car. We are walking along the freeway. I am thinking to myself, "Why would I or anyone else buy her car if she does not even drive it herself? There must be something wrong with the car."

We are now at a hotel in Las Vegas, where we are given an executive VIP suite. I do not want a big room because I think it is arrogant and pompous. I am a simple person of common means. I see the drug addict guy again. I am tired of running into him all the time. I am surprised that he is still alive. He should be dead by now. I notice that I can now see the inside of his stomach. It looks like he might be infested with those alien termites. I am thinking, "Die already, get it over with." I start banging my fist on him, trying to put an end to him once and for all.

The struggle woke me up all of a sudden and again, someone pinched me. Thinking it might be that hand again, I turned to look toward the closet door to see if I could see anything. Instead of the hand, I saw my grandmother who passed away when I was in elementary school. She was standing beside the closet door with her apron on and those cute grandma shoes she used to wear with the stockings halfway up her calves. She is looking at me crossly and giving me the universal signal for "No," a "No" sign with her index finger, while holding a large wooden serving spoon in the other hand.

I love it when I am able to see my long deceased family and friends in my visions and dreams. It gives me the assurance that they are still with me. It makes life just a little bit easier and places a bounce in my step. We have all made a few bad choices in our lives that have brought with them painful experiences. Those experiences are necessary and serve a purpose -- to teach us a valuable lesson required to prepare us and move us along to the next step in our journey. We often grit our teeth just long enough to get through the experience and then make a run from it in an effort of avoid looking at the root underlying issue that needs to change within our awareness. We must resolve to move through the experiences we leave behind and not simply run past them. We cannot run from ourselves. A dry drunk is a dry drunk. We must look at what we are running from. We must sit with ourselves.

I then fell back asleep and once again, in a different scene, found myself running from some people who were after me. I am avoiding them as if my life depends on it. I feel like the Pac Man constantly, on the run and never having any rest. The terrain is treacherous and some roads I fear have dead ends.

In despair and feeling my options were closing in on me, I woke up suddenly. Above my head I could see a spiraling blue vortex. There was blue angel hair everywhere. I looked around and sure enough, five blue luminescent figures were standing at the foot of my bed. I shied away from them, pulling the covers slightly over my head. I heard the man in the center say to me, "Why do you avoid me?" I squirmed for an out. I just could not deal with this right now. The spirit persisted, telling me in a stern voice that they were my spirit guides and they wanted my attention. They needed me to pay attention. They needed me to fulfill my purpose. They said I needed to make changes in my life. They spoke to me not in words, but somehow telepathically. The language was not English, yet I understood their message. I felt very forgetful.

My short-term memory was non-existent so everything they said basically went in one ear and out the other. I kept asking them to tell me again, to tell me exactly what they wanted from me and what I was supposed to do. They indicated their patience and repeated part of what they had just said. Of course, none of it stuck.

As I looked at their faces, I somehow recognized them, but not from this lifetime. They knew me very well. They each took turns telling me who they were and asked different questions for me to ponder over. I was amazed at the clarity with which I saw their faces. They wanted me to know that they were not figments of my imagination. I was not dreaming. One touched me, grabbing my knee to shake it. I jumped a mile high in my bed. I had no choice but to acknowledge them as real. They would not allow me to deny their existence any longer. One of them, I understood, was there representing my inner child. He looked to be around 14 years old with lots of curly black hair on his head. He was very wise and knew so much. He kept asking me, "Why are you doing this? Why do you run?"

I then saw the color of the angel hair around me change and become very prominent. Another group of people appeared and they each took turns talking to me. The colors shifted again and now green was the prominent color. A third set of people appeared, with each spirit pausing to talk to me. I was so nervous and scared; I did not remember a thing they said.

Dream work opens the door to a host of unseen experiences. We all incarnate with a purpose and goal to achieve in each lifetime we find ourselves in. It is a contract we hold with our Higher Self. How we go about achieving that purpose is entirely up to us. In some cases, we need to settle the score on the karmic baggage we have been running from, which we acquired in previous lifetimes. It is something we decide for ourselves long before we are born. At some deep level, I know my contribution to the understanding of dreams is in some way the manner in which I chose to give back to humanity and repay some debt I incurred and have been running from. This will allow my spirit to be set free. Our spirit guides and guardian angels, and we do have them, are simply there to help us remember why we are here and to remind us of our purpose and original intent, for the lives in which we have presence in time.

Wrestling With the House of David

Last night while lying in bed, I began my normal pre-sleep meditation. *I quickly dropped into a dream where I found myself wrestling with another man. I am struggling with determination. I am not going to let him overcome me.*

The struggle was so intense that I suddenly woke up out of the dream. I looked up and floating above my head was my opponent. He looked at me with the eyes of love. The robe he wore appeared Greek; cinched about his waist, I could see the pleats of his robe beneath his arm. He said, "Why do you struggle with me?" His eyes were filled with tenderness; they were the eyes of a gentle lover. He then said to me, "You are of the house of David."

His image soon faded and all I could remember were his soulful eyes. On my way to work, I tried to reflect on the meaning of the vision and dream. I closed my eyes to meditate. I began seeing beautiful billowing white clouds with blue outlines. I knew it was an image from Heaven. Could this man with whom I had wrestled be David from the Bible? In pondering the question, I heard a voice say, "I am David." "Wow," I thought. "I had better go back and re-read all of the biblical accounts of David to see if I can glean any hidden message from this vision."

David is depicted as the most righteous of all the kings of Israel. In response to David's desire to build a House of God, God promised David that his royal house would endure forever.

The path of self-discovery is so amazing. Every day brings a new mystery. I learned that this is the David who wrestled with Goliath. Like David, we too must wrestle with our Goliaths in coming to find out who we are. The house of God is within us. We are the house of David.

Angels and Spirit Guides

What's Beyond the Blue Veil?

When I first began to see spirits following my near death experience, I did not know if I was hallucinating, going crazy or actually seeing real spirits. Then too, I was not only dreaming about aliens but was also seeing the spirits of aliens just like I was seeing human spirits. I was obviously terrified and not quite sure what was going on within me. Before I understood what was actually happening, my fear projections had the best of me. For a time, I truly believed we were being invaded by aliens.

The process of awakening can be a very frightening experience until we get a grip and understand what it is we are seeing. I hope that by sharing my experience here, it will turn the negative into a positive and make it just a little less painful and frightening for everyone who will go through this process. My reference to aliens here and throughout this book is symbolic and in no way addresses whether aliens truly exist in our Universe. My suspicion is that we are those aliens.

What is the connection between aliens, angels and spirit guides? The answer for me was an incomplete picture. In my experience, spirits (including angels) manifest as vibratory energy much like the heat from a jet engine. From my observation, it appears that spirits of the recently deceased have a vibration that is closer to ours and therefore more easily perceived when our vibration is raised in meditation or through dreams. The vibration of our angels and spirit guides is often significantly higher than that of deceased relatives, with some of their vibratory energy being beyond the range that normal meditation or dream states can perceive. Therefore what results is an incomplete picture. The reason I know this is because I have seen the transformation of energy go from alien to angel as my fears lessened and my ability to increase my own vibration improved. In addition, the mind has a way of trying to complete the picture for you and uses your thought projections to do so. If you are in a state of fear, your mind is going to complete the picture by projecting that fear and associating it with the partial image.

As time went by and I became more assured and confident that there was truly nothing to be afraid of and no harm was going to come to me, the images of the aliens began to change. In time, I was able to see them clearly for who they really are; beautiful loving angelic beings here to support us like loving parents who watch their children play on the school playground. The aliens turned out to be nothing more than the fears I had held and projected upon my many guardian angels and spirit guides.

In addition, there are many other realms where there exist energy forms of all kinds including the energy forms of the faeries. Not everything you will encounter is human in form. We are not all that there is. God's thought forms are diverse in expression yet their essence is the same. Even with these, there is nothing to fear when we anchor ourselves firmly in the presence of Love as we remain true to our own essence.

I had a dream where I found myself at a singles party. I am wandering around the place not knowing why I am there. People there are meeting people and socializing left and right but I am not finding anyone to match up with. Someone at the party asks me why I am so tense. He tells me that the best way to benefit from these social gatherings is to just let go. Not quite happy with that bit of advice, I continue wandering around looking for someone

ANGELS AND SPIRIT GUIDES

with whom I might hit it off. I then find a VIP area that is roped off behind a blue veil. I can see through the slits in the veil. It looks like people are enjoying themselves within this VIP section. Feeling left out, I want to be allowed access into this area but I do not believe that I am a VIP cardholding member. I then walk around back and find an opening within the VIP area that is unattended. I walk in and find that the guys on this side of the blue veil are in training for the Gay Rainbow Olympics. All the guys here are in tip top condition and at the prime of their life. They are all wearing vivid blue full body tights that appear to have an inner neon glow. I am amazed that they are not even interested in the activities going on within the singles area; they are simply content within themselves. The guys are doing summersaults over my head like acrobats. I feel totally out of place because I am not an athlete of any kind. I head back toward the opening to leave and before exiting I pause to look back at all the colorful blue gymnasts. I think to myself, "If I had only started young, I too could have been a gay Olympic athlete."

The first experience associated with my awakening was my sudden ability to see the colored night lights as I lay in bed at night meditating. I know these lights now to be the Christ Light within me that produces an inner glow. This began to happen about six months before having my near death experience. Blue was the first color I saw. Along with the night lights there appeared to be a dense etheric fog that seemed to serve as veil of separation, like a sheer curtain that separated the spiritual from the physical. For a long time, I saw vague shadowy images just beyond the veil that looked like people or spirits going about their celestial business but I was not quite sure if they were real or if I simply had an over-active imagination. In time, I was allowed to pierce through the blue veil and see clearly the spirit world that lay just beyond it. I believe I was given this dream so that I could not only see what was beyond but also to understand how to find my original dream.

In the Course of a Dream Emanuel for Love

I have always searched for something or someone that would make me complete, never feeling quite important enough. Here I learned that all I need to do is let go and leave behind my preconceived notions of what it is that I expect to get or have. There is a different way to live. Instead of looking outside myself, I can look deep within me, beyond the blue veil to the original vision with which I incarnated into this lifetime; to the dream I once had for my life. To find our way back here is to create within ourselves a place where we can truly experience peace, joy, happiness and fulfillment. It is within this space and vision that I hold my personal VIP status. We are all VIP members with a unique purpose and spiritual gift which no one else can duplicate. There is no one holding us back or restricting our access. On the contrary, there are many spirits beyond the blue veil who are in support of us, training alongside us.

In spirit, I am always at the prime of my life. It is in this space that we can truly realize our full potential and train to perform summersaults like an Olympic athlete. We were meant to be rainbow Olympians. We are part of an Olympic team with a shared dream and vision. We can be content within ourselves by moving into this vision and remembering our original dream; to be an Olympian and participate in an Olympic dream. If we hold fast to the vision and do the necessary training to support our shared vision, the universe will work out the details allowing us to manifest our dreams. Dreams were truly meant to come true.

A Lecture from Martha on Staying Clean

I had a dream that I was in the back room of my house alone, using. I had retreated to a corner of the room and could not come out to face life.

ANGELS AND SPIRIT GUIDES

I am hearing activity in the other rooms of the house but the drugs are keeping me in fear, paralyzed and unable to face what is out there. For a long time, I sit in the corner of the room. I finally cannot deny that people are in my house. I must do the right thing and leave my corner to see who it is and what they are doing in my house. I open the door and walk cautiously over to the front bedroom. I notice the house is now completely empty of all furniture and is thoroughly clean. The hardwood floors are polished and spotless. Could it be that I hid for so long that they forgot I existed and have moved on and are now making the house available to another occupant? I look out the front window and can see down below where they have packed all my clothes in boxes and are getting ready to haul my stuff away.

Scared, I turn and look toward my bed. A woman I do not know is now sleeping in my bed with her face turned away. I cannot believe that someone else is already living and sleeping in my bed. I run back to the bedroom where I have been in seclusion for so long. As I walk in, I notice this room has also now been cleaned of all the mess I left behind. The room is now completely clean and empty of all furniture. The floors are immaculate with a high gloss finish. I am told that my house is now being rented as offices for housing the homeless. A guy escorts me through the rooms of what used to be my house. Even though it is for a good cause, it is very unsettling to see it occupied by someone other than me. As I walk through the rooms the workers turn and look at me. I feel as if I am an apparition in what used to be my home.

The unsettled feeling jarred me awake. I looked around and noticed beside me the image of the woman I had seen sleeping in my bed. She had a very distinctive look that reminded me of Martha Stewart with sandy blond shoulder length hair. She had a strand of hair that kept falling down over her face, slightly covering her left eye. She was looking at me and talking to me. I could see her lips move but I could not hear her voice. At some level, I knew she was lecturing me and explaining the dream in which I had found myself.

Somehow, I understood. Not wanting to hear what she was telling me, I closed my eyes and immediately returned to the dream. After just a few minutes, I decided to open my eyes and check to see if she was gone. I opened my eyes only to find her still standing there having a discussion with me. Looking at her, I was amazed at the amount of detail with which she appeared before me; not one facial feature was omitted.

I then closed my eyes and returned to the dream. I was in one of the rooms where employees were gawking at me. I felt like a displaced apparition appearing in their world. Feeling uncomfortable and totally out of place, I opened my eyes again and left the dream, but somehow the people who were gawking at me in the dream were now in front of me. I could not escape their eyes whether mine were opened or closed. I had no choice but to face what was in front of me. After a few minutes of feeling their presence, their faces began to fade in and out like reflections in a pond. Knowing I had to return to the dream, I decided to just go back to sleep and deal with whatever the dream was trying to teach me.

I find myself back in one of the rooms of the house that is now a copy room. I see a ream of paper and one of those guns they use to stamp prices on merchandise. I think I am going to grab this price gun and make as if I am an employee and try to walk right out the front door unnoticed. I make it out of the copy room with my price gun and into the next room but people in the house begin to notice me as I try to make my getaway. I see people coming toward me to confront me as if I am a patient in a psyche ward. They have a look of determination on their faces. Panicked, I begin to fly to try to avoid these people. I feel like I am in a Wal-Mart or discount store floating among the rafters. Above their heads they are stringing a net to try to catch me like a bird in flight. I manage to escape their net. In the distance, I see an open skylight from where I can escape. As I approach the skylight, I notice that it is snowing outside. Fearing I will be worse off freezing to death, I surrender to the rooms of the house and lay down my price gun.

Dream work promises a better way of resolving our karmic patterns. Through dream work a day will come when we will awaken and find that everything has changed. We are no longer the same person we used to be. What we held on to for so long no longer serves us. We will be able to shed those old things we identified with and move on with a new and honorable purpose. This dream confirmed to me what I already knew, namely, that my spirit guides sleep with me and use my dreams to teach me what I need to do to set my house in order and pay the karmic debt I have incurred, in the most efficient way possible. Eventually we must face ourselves in the copy room of our life, where we are allowed to take inventory and set our price. There is a way out and it lies in surrendering to the process of self-inquiry.

My Guardian Angel Watches Over Me

> *"Angel of God, my guardian dear*
> *To whom his love commits me here*
> *Ever this day be at my side*
> *To light to guard to rule and guide"*

I frequently recite this prayer I learned in Sunday school. I know today there has always been an angel close by watching over me.

IN THE COURSE OF A DREAM EMANUEL FOR LOVE

I woke up suddenly from a troubling dream and I could not fall back to sleep. I lay quietly in my bed reciting my prayers and staring off into the darkness of my bedroom. With my eyes open, I began to see a bluish green light descending from above. Angel hair soon filled my bedroom. It was everywhere, vibrating with radiant color and covering my comforter. I watched it in amazement. I then saw an angel descend from above. She had golden hair and wore a radiant white flowing robe. I was mesmerized as I watched her descend. Just before she came to rest beside my bed, she lifted and spread wide her wings so as to cushion her landing. I did not say a word. The room was dark with just a little bit of light coming in from the street. Now the room glowed with the light of my angelic visitor. I thought I dare not move. She then walked over beside me and tucked my covers in along my side. Her loving dark brown eyes looked down at me as her long golden hair draped and touched my sheets. With her touch, I felt her blessing. Our eyes met and she knew I was aware of her presence. She had a face so beautiful and radiant and a look that only my mother could give me, a look that said, "I love you." Her image slowly faded, leaving behind the vibrating and glowing angel hair. Curious, I reached out across my comforter and scooped some of it up between the palms of my hands. I held my palms together as in prayer. In complete and utter amazement my hands were glowing. I slowly pulled my palms apart and as I did the angel hair created a membrane like cellophane between my palms, which reflected my image like unto a mirror. As I gazed at my reflection in this celestial mirror, my face suddenly began to transform and change right before my very eyes. I was undergoing a transfiguration. I was being shown every face I ever bore in all my many lifetimes. Face upon face -- some male -- some female -- of all nationalities -- and in each face, though not my own, I recognized myself. Every single one of them I knew beyond a shadow of a doubt to be me.

As surely as I recognize my own face in my bathroom mirror, I recognized these faces to be me.

How would your life change if you knew angels do in fact exist? If they told you to look for them in your dreams, would you make the effort to remember them? If you knew that you were in fact connected to every living thing on the inside, would you see your neighbor and the environment in which you live differently? If you knew that you had lived many different lives and bore the face of every nationality, both male and female, both rich and poor, would you look upon a foreigner or stranger in your land differently? If you knew that we are, without exception, One in the mind of God and that this God is One across all creation and across every religion, would you look across religious boundaries differently? I know this to be true because I have seen it reflected within me. It is undeniably self-evident. One need only look within oneself for the truth.

Day Spirits and Night Spirits - The Hidden Messages and the Winning Lotto Numbers

This night, I had one of the most incredible dream adventures ever. The dreams I had were by far the most vivid I have ever experienced. I was totally lucid the entire night. I even remember thinking to myself that I was going to wake up tired if I did not shut my mind off and go to sleep. Luckily, with the initial thought came a rebuttal, "How do you know you are going to be tired if you've never experienced this degree of lucidity before?" I decided I was going to allow myself the adventure.

IN THE COURSE OF A DREAM EMANUEL FOR LOVE

The adventure took place all in one night but within that night, I had several false awakenings and several dream days and nights in which I had sub-dreams where I was also lucid in the sub-dreams. I encountered day spirits and night spirits. It became so confusing that I constantly had to test to see if what I was experiencing was a dream or reality. Through working with my dreams, I have learned several techniques for testing the dream, such as looking at my watch, or trying to make eye contact with people, or reading street signs. The dreams this time were so real that I had a considerable amount of difficulty in being able to tell whether it was a dream or not. At one point, I had a false awakening where I was with Joe. His image was so perfect that I could not tell him apart from reality. I lived out several sub-days and sub-nights in which I had sub-dreams and during those days I shared with this "dream Joe" the substance of my sub-dreams.

In one of the sub-dreams, I could see night spirits whom I believed were base spirits. They would come around and try to misguide me.

The night is overcrowded with night spirits. It feels as if we are all in a busy nightclub. I can see all the translucent spirits trying to impose themselves on me. I try to ward them away by showing them my crucifix, which I wear around my neck. Some are brazen and provoking fear in me. I cannot overcome them.

The day comes and with it come the day spirits to guide me. I do not know who to trust but I remember reading about the tactics of the base and demonic spirits and I know that the dark spirits do not like the light, so I choose to trust the day spirits on this fact alone.

The day spirits are teaching me how to walk through the night without being affected by the trappings of the night. I learn that God prohibits the dark spirits from being able to touch us. They can come right up on us to incite fear through intimidation but they cannot touch us if we do not engage them or invite them in.

Angels and Spirit Guides

The next night, the night spirits come out in search of me to lure me into the dark of night. They take me to a crowded bar. I try hard not to engage them and to just make it through the night. I become disoriented and cannot tell if this is a dream anymore so I ask one of the translucent dark spirits at the bar what city we are in. He replies sarcastically, "What do you mean, what city are we in? We are in Cora. Where did you think we were?" Without giving anything away, I play it off as though I know where Cora is. I know by his sarcasm that he is a dark spirit and that I am dreaming.

I then realize I have wings. If I have wings then that must mean I can fly my way out of the crowd and away from Cora. I see a skylight up in the ceiling and so I make a run for it. Not knowing how to fly with my wings, I just will it and off I go. I head for the blue skylight and into the day.

With the day come the day spirits to teach me more. A woman spirit comes to me who is wearing nurse scrubs with the colors pastel green, white and pastel peachy orange. The colors strike me to be a very odd choice but I assume they are the colors associated with the day spirits. This is how I will know them. She then proceeds to tell me that she is going to escort me the following night and teach me how to walk the night. She instructs me to stay close to her at all times.

The night comes and I follow her closely. When the crowds come, I am quickly overwhelmed and lose my day spirit in the crowd. I think, "Oh no, I'm lost among the base spirits." The base spirits try to lure me back into the nightclub, but I stand outside the club, feeling lost and not wanting to go in. I then hear a voice from above call to me, "Ruben, over here." I look around and cannot see who is calling me. With all the confusion, I cannot even remember what my day spirit guide looks like. I hear the voice again but this time I pay attention to where it is coming from. It sounds like it is coming from upstairs inside my head. I look up and above me is my day spirit floating above my head. She waves down to me and gives me an indication that she was at all times with me.

Suddenly I awoke in real life; my *real* life. Baffled and confused, I wondered what was going on. I looked around my bedroom. Yes, I was really awake. I then looked up, and above my head I could see the vibration of angel hair. Within the angel hair was the translucent image of my day spirit floating above me. I had a funny feeling this was going to turn into a precognitive dream. Excited to find out, I quickly closed my eyes to return to dream land knowing I was in good hands with my day spirit close by.

I fell back asleep and found myself in the bar once again among the base spirits. Once again, I become disoriented and cannot tell whether I am in a dream or not. I think, "What now?" I feel lost and confused again. Then from above I hear a familiar voice say, "Over here, Ruben." As I turn to look, I hear myself snore. I chuckle within myself, knowing the snore is coming from me. I know then that I am dreaming. I will myself to rise to the level where the angelic voice is coming from.

Suddenly, I am in the upper decks of a stadium observing what is going on down below me. I am told the base spirits are limited in their ability to see. They are unable to see above their heads. Their vision is one-dimensional so they do not even realize that they are constantly being watched. I then ascend higher into the stadium. As I climb higher, I begin to hear the voice of a lecturer or university instructor delivering a lecture to internists, as if I were in a teaching hospital. We are doctors watching and learning new medical procedures. I am then shown my life from above. I cannot believe I am so close to the "me" down below. The "me" below is not even aware that the "me" above is watching over me.

I then see a dark spirit come into the room and it looks up at me. I am shocked. How did it know to look up? The entity is completely black void of any light and he wants to claim me. He calls out in a guttural tone, "He's mine!" My day spirits turn me around and take me by the hand and show me a commercial where they have a secret message hidden for me to take back. They tell me to pay close attention to the video tape that they are going to

ANGELS AND SPIRIT GUIDES

play. It will be in slow motion so that I will see the hidden message. I see an advertisement for three different fast foods. In the video tape on instant replay is a white message that flashes on the screen. They zoom in on the message and I can see that it contains numbers. The message is hidden in the numbers. They are lottery numbers. I am told that they are the winning lotto numbers and if I take them back with me I can win the lottery and be set for life. I do not think I can commit all the numbers to memory so I commit to memory the last three digits of the lotto numbers. They are 815. I am then given a small piece of angelic bread. It is a translucent piece of bread. At first, I am hesitant to eat this spiritual bread but I eat it as they instruct.

I then find myself back at the bar. I want to get out of the bar so I walk out the front door and find myself on the sidewalk. I look at the cars passing by and notice that all the cars have a small tiny blue headlight below the front bumper. It appears to be a small pin-sized third eye. Every car that passes by has this little blue headlight in the center. I think to myself, "Since when did everyone awaken their third eye? I thought I was the only one who was awake to the third eye phenomena."

I then find myself sitting down as a child playing with my wireless remote controlled car. My little wireless car also has a small third headlight. Suddenly a second car comes into my playground. Its headlights are even bigger than mine and it too has a third headlight that is much bigger than mine. It is a better model of car than mine with increased vision capability and better maneuvering. The headlights are deep emerald green. I think it might want to overpower my little car, so I grab the newcomer car and turn it upside down so it will not threaten my little car. Upside down it is forced to sit still until I can figure out where it came from and what to do with it.

I then have a false awakening and I share my dream of the lotto numbers with my dream Joe. People are suspicious of my abilities in this day and think me to be a criminal because I seem to have inside information. I see the police coming to my door and the choppers hovering overhead. I tell Joe I have foreseen this and I know they are coming to try and falsely accuse me.

When the police enter I know they are coming for me because I have the winning lotto numbers. I tell the officer that I saw all this transpire on the Learning Channel the night before. He says, "What Learning Channel? There was no special last night." I then realize they are unaware of the Learning Channel so I just play it off, telling him I saw something similar somewhere else.

They then go to search the house and I quietly tell Joe under my breath, "Remember the winning lotto numbers." They cannot find anything on me so they drop the charges. I then win the lottery as foretold. When I receive my winnings they come in a luminescent blue bag. I know I cannot keep them so I go outside and toss it up in the air.

This dream showed me that there are base spirits who by their choices remain locked in their own karma. This limits their ability to see beyond the dimension in which they find themselves. Unable to see above their heads, they are led to believe the illusion that there is nothing beyond what they can see. This holds true for many of us in the physical world of three dimensions and those in the next dimension above us. We can call it the 4th dimension or astral plane. However we care to refer to it, we have, for the most part, failed to look up. Base spirits, those locked in karmic patterns, are like us, limited in what they are aware of and in disbelief of what they cannot see. Lacking faith and insight, they engage in power struggles to control and dominate the 3rd and 4th dimensions. This leads them to the trappings of the dark night of the soul. We already have within us the ability to recognize the characteristics of the night. Those who do not awaken cannot see that there are spiritual planes of higher enlightenment above them, watching over them and ready and able to help them tap into the universal force and realize their dreams. Our day spirits, those spirit guides and angels who come to assist us, are present with us all the time whenever we need them.

There is much we will encounter in the dream space, some of which might be very frightening, but we can be completely assured that we have God's watchful eye of protection and our celestial guides with us during the entire process. God is with us always.

We are here for the experience of remembering who and what we truly are. The process of remembering comes by faith in the unseen God and the belief in our oneness. We all must learn how to walk the night and recognize the illusions for what they are; illusions. Recognizing illusions gives us the ability to fly with a mere thought and become fully aware of the higher realms. We can break free of our self-imposed limitations and ascend higher into the stadium of our minds. We can become university instructors, teaching and learning. We realize there are no limits to what we can do when we break free. To rise above and see ourselves through the Observer, the Higher Self, the Holy Spirit, is to become aware of our true essence.

I believe the dark spirit who looked up at me was my shadow self; one of the demons we allow to take up residence within us. We have allowed the shadows of the ego to run our lives and stake claims to who we are. Their existence and expression is threatened when we turn our focus away from the dark night. They only exist as long as we allow them use of our energy.

We contain within us the winning lotto numbers that make up the code and key to awakening our DNA. We are seeds that have sprouted but have yet to penetrate through the surface and reach upward into the light to grow to our full potential. We are unlocking the door through which we feed our souls with spiritual bread that we may grow in fullness and purpose of who we were meant to be. We can be set for life upon discovering the code we each hold within us.

In the Course of a Dream Emanuel for Love

No one can do the work for you. No minister or religious guru can teach you what is within you to discover. Religion only serves to start you on your path. Religion was not meant to hold the end all or final doctrine. It was the shell from which we were born. The Bible ends with the Book of Revelation, which is itself entirely a collection of dreams and visions. Where Religions end the Dream begins.

Awakening our third eye, our center of Christ Consciousness, provides us with better vision and the necessary awareness to make better choices that are more in line with our soul's purpose. We will achieve our full potential because we see the bigger picture and the interplay of the lightbearers upon a common universal goal. We turn that vision in on itself by sitting still though meditation and dream work. This helps color our world with the light and essence of spirit within, bringing heaven to our earthly existence. Doing this allows us to hit the lotto jackpot and live out our original dream by creating Heaven on Earth.

This dream did turn out to be precognitive. I had a make-up session with my therapist this morning, which we had decided to have at his house instead of in his office. It was the first time I had ever been to his house. He had agreed to squeeze me in that weekend. I arrived a few minutes early so I sat in my car reviewing my voice recording of the dream to make sure I had not missed anything. The colors my day spirit was wearing kept popping into my head. Of all the colors possible, why would my dreaming mind choose pastel green, pastel peachy orange and white? "Who in the world would pick such a funky color palette?" I thought to myself. I also kept hearing the words from the dream, "You will know them by these colors."

I wrapped things up with my voice recorder and proceeded to walk up to my therapist's house. I rang the doorbell and he promptly came to the door. As he opened his front door, there in front of me was his foyer and living room. His living room was done in a pastel green with white trim and the foyer was a pastel peachy orange with white trim. This was a dream come true. I knew there would be a message in today's session from my day spirit, channeled through my therapist, without him even knowing it.

I withheld telling him about the dream and the synchronicity of his choice of colors. During the session he oddly enough suggested that I seek out a metaphysical church and start attending. He even went so far as suggesting one that he was aware of in his neighborhood. I took that suggestion to be the voice of my day spirit telling me to follow the suggested lead given to me. I knew somehow that seeking out that church would steer me down the path that I needed to travel for my highest good. My therapist had been teaching me about the Enneagram. I knew that working with him on my "5" personality type of the Enneagram would help me improve my spiritual condition.

From this dream I also started to look at numbers more closely. Is there some hidden truth in numbers? Why did my dreaming mind choose specifically the last three numbers to focus on, as if those three numbers held the complete truth? I looked at the numbers 815 and learned that the numerological equivalence is $8+1+5 = 14$ and $1 + 4 = 5$. My winning lotto number is 5. 5 is the number of my Enneagram.

The Door Is Ajar

I had a dream where I owned a large white SUV, something big like an Expedition. As I get into the drivers seat, I notice through the rear view window that the left side passenger door is open. My first thought is "I'm glad someone didn't find their way into my unattended vehicle." I then think, "I had better close the door." I could do one of two things, either speed off fast and allow the forward motion of the car to close the door, or do the right thing and get up out of the car and walk over to close the door. I decide to do the right thing and get out of my car and walk around the vehicle to close the door. I take a final look at the rear view mirror before getting out and notice there is now a young woman seated in the 3rd row seat of the car that I had not noticed before. Wondering if my eyes are playing tricks on me, I come in close to the mirror to study the image of this mystery woman. She appears to be transparent. All I can see is her silhouette and the outlines of her features.

Somewhat irritated that I now have a homeless person squatting in the back seat of my SUV, I instruct her to get out of the car. I walk around the car to escort her out of the vehicle. Complaining under her breath, she complies with my request. To my surprise, behind her is a second young woman followed by a third. I am thinking, "Where were they all hiding that I didn't see any of them?"

I tell them the vehicle is mine and I want them out of my car. They are reluctant to leave. The first woman tells me that as soon as I drive off they will all be right back in the car with me.

I reply, "NO YOU WON'T."

She replies, "OH YES WE WILL, WE CAN WALK FASTER THAN YOU CAN DRIVE THAT CAR."

I turn around, shut the doors and get in my car to drive off. I am fumbling, trying to find the power door locks to secure myself in the vehicle. I give up finding the door locks and simply drive off. Unfortunately there are people walking down the middle of the street blocking traffic. It occurs to me that the woman had a point all along; they can walk faster than I can drive.

God takes many forms even though we are often not aware of His presence. There is nothing better than having an angel for a back seat driver. While the door is ajar, God is with us. If we allow God in, we avail ourselves of the wisdom of the universe. We find that the universe knows much more than we do. It is not that God orchestrates our lives; we still sit in the driver's seat. God is only there to ensure our safety and help guide us along the path we choose for ourselves. We cannot secure our lives without God, and to secure our lives requires that we awaken and allow God's guiding presence in the car.

In Case You Need Me, Speed Dial 4 on Your Cell Phone

I am at a county fair where we are guests at a hotel. One of the rooms in the hotel has dining tables that are laid out with orange and red tablecloths. Each table has a center piece that is garnished with pieces of dried fruit. Adjacent to this room is an outdoor white cloth tent where they store fruit that they have grown organically. Each type of fruit is stored in its own personal wooden crate. It reminds me of something you might see displayed at Pottery Barn, except that at Pottery Barn they might be selling fruit scented candles individually packed in their own little crates.

By force of habit, I take the bug spray and spray the fruit. I am told that I do not need to do that because the fruit grown here does not have bugs. I am thinking I might have spoiled their organic crop. I realize my mistake and quickly discard the bug spray. Far away in an adjacent tent, I can see that there is a black lioness who is giving birth to her cub.

I felt a tap on my shoulder which caused me to awaken suddenly. As I opened my eyes, beside me was the figure of an old bearded man who sat in a lotus position on my bed. I instantly recognized the man to be Sri Yukteswar, who was the Guru of Paramahansa Yogananda, who in turn was the founder of the Self Realization Fellowship. I was a student of SRF many years ago when I first ventured away from my Christian upbringing. I had studied with them for about two years but never went through with their Kriya Yoga initiation. It was through the lessons of SRF and their many references back to the Bible and other scriptures that gave me a renewed and fresh appreciation for scripture. They helped me recognize God as one and the same across all religions.

Sri Yukteswar began talking to me about the universe and how the number of the universe was 4. I could clearly see his lips moving but I heard no sound. I laid there puzzled, wondering why of all people Sri Yukteswar. I could understand finding Paramahansa on my bed but not Sri Yukteswar. I knew very little about him other than that he was Paramahansa's Guru. He kept talking and talking and making facial expressions. I kept trying to tell him in my mind that I could not hear him.

"I can't hear you; I can only see your lips move."

He would respond, "Yes you can."

I would tell him again, "No, I'm sorry but I can't hear you; I can only see your lips moving."

He would patiently reply yet again, "Yes, you can hear me."

Looking back in hindsight, I realize that even though I did not hear anything audibly with my ears, I did apparently receive his message telepathically, otherwise how would I have known what his responses were and his message to me about the properties of the universe. I did not know how that bit of information would help me until much later when it became apparent that much meaning is hidden in astrology and numerology.

He finally faded and I rolled over and fell back to sleep. A couple hours later, I awoke suddenly to again find him standing beside my bed asking me for the time. I looked at my wrist watch but since I was not wearing my glasses, I could not read the time on my watch. Instead, I held out my arm and tapped my index finger on the face of my watch, indicating for him to look at it for himself. He apparently did not want to make the effort himself to look at it but instead wanted me to tell him the time. Knowing he was not going to leave me alone until I told him the time, I sat up in bed to look over at my alarm clock, which sat on the nightstand on the other side of my bed. The digital clock read 5:45am. "It's 5:45am."

This was the morning for sudden awakenings because for a third time I would be roused yet again and with magic and grace given a code by which I would confirm the existence of my guardian angel. I had been in a dream where I was with a group of friends. One of my friends named Jennifer had taken a special interest in me. (In real life, I do not have a friend named Jennifer) She gave me a cell phone that had her phone number preprogrammed in it so that I could call upon her any time I needed her for any reason. She then showed me how, by simply pushing a single button, it would autodial and connect me with her.

As I was standing there with her, she pushed the button to test the phone. In that same moment in real life, I awoke suddenly. Without even thinking, I reached over to grab my voice recorder to record the details of the dream I had just had regarding the preprogrammed cell phone. As I got to the part where I recorded, "....and she tested it by pushing the button like this," my real phone on my nightstand rang. The sound of the phone ringing was captured on my voice recorder. I did not answer it because it was too early in the morning so I assumed it had to be a wrong number. I also did not correlate the testing of the preprogrammed cell phone with the synchronicity of my real phone ringing at precisely the same time.

It was not until later that day when I went to journal my dream into my computer that I replayed my voice recording and heard the phone ringing in the background. Then the synchronicity behind it all hit me. Mysteriously, ever since then whenever I have dreamt about my guardian angel and have gone to journal the dream, the message indicator on my cell phone would beep to let me know that I have a message. It would beep at precisely the right time and not as a result of having been moved such that it had come into cell range.

I did not know if my cell phone was faulty, but it could go the entire day and not beep at all to let me know that I have a message. It always beeped at precisely the right time to let me know my guardian angel was with me.

We are the fruit of the vine. We are spirit having a human experience. That experience can never adversely affect our spirit no matter what it is that we experience. We are bug-proof. Our fruit may dry and be boxed away but our mother, the lioness, is continually giving birth to its cubs.

Since that dream, I have learned from one of my spirit guides that Jennifer, whose name is actually Guinevere (which means "white fay" or "white ghost"), is in fact my guardian angel. I have one spirit guide named Felicity who is around me all the time. She reminds me of my older sister. She has shoulder length straight hair and short bangs down to her eyebrows. Her hair curls forward as it comes to rest upon her shoulders. She has a signature trait of closing her eyes and softly shaking her head from side to side like in the shampoo commercials. In the etheric world, her hair moves with great body and bounce as if in slow motion. Every time I see her, she does her signature move as it has a way of pacifying me.

As I am sure you might be wondering, I would like to share here how I came to know their names. For a long time, I did not know. I just recognized my spirit guides as nameless, simply having seen them before. It happened one day in a guided meditation that was ironically titled, "Channeling Your Spirit Guides." While focused inward on my third eye in that meditation, I had a vision where my spirit guide came and did the little thing she always does with her hair. I had my headphones on, listening to the guided meditation, and on the recording as if on queue it said, "If you should see any of your spirit guides simply ask them their name." So I did. To my surprise, I heard a voice say, "My name is Felicity."

Shocked, yet knowing I had to take advantage of this moment, I asked her to please also tell me the name of my guardian angel, to which I heard the voice say, "Don't you remember? Her name is Jennifer and she is the one that calls you on the phone."

I had not equated Jennifer with an angel. In the dream she appeared simply as a person and not as an angel. Recalling the memory of Jennifer from the dream and the times when my guardian angel had appeared, it suddenly rang true. I had a moment of clarity and I remembered all the places I had seen her in visions and dreams and I knew Felicity was telling the truth. She was the same person.

Angels do not always appear in visions or dreams in their winged form. They come to teach a lesson and will appear in whatever form necessary to carry the intended message. One must look to the soul of the person or spirit to know who is there.

My Guardian Angel Takes Me to the Filming of Night Bright

My spirit guides have learned exactly how to wake me up. Tonight, I woke up in the middle of the night swinging my arms. When I opened my eyes, there was a woman at my feet kneeling with her head bowed down. She looked like a gypsy with many glowing colors. She was the embodiment of my inner night lights. Her eyes were glowing with a lavender color and glittery pearl eye shadow. Her hair was jet black with tiny specs of silver glitter that reminded me of the night sky. Her eyes illuminated my bed sheets and the glitter cast specks of light like stars on the walls and ceiling of my bedroom. As soon as I saw her and the magnificent glow of her eyes, I paused so as not to startle her. She remained still, casting her eyes and her glow upon my bed. Her eyes were like amethyst crystal gems in the night; the color of my birth stone.

The vision faded and I laid back down and began dreaming that I was in a dark warehouse that had been converted into a movie studio.

I feel like Batman in his bat cave in Gotham City. There are reels and reels of blue 3M magnetic tape. The tape is like painter's tape, blue on one side and black on the other. There are ashes all over the ground. As I gaze at the ashes, the ashes become white as snow. The studio people are showing me all the different cameras they use to film the movies. There are many little people there; Munchkins perhaps. It reminds me of Disneyland's, "It's A Small World." The colors in the cave are so vibrant, like nothing I have ever seen. I lose myself in the colors and begin to float with my head back among the daisies and other flowers. It is a kaleidoscope of colors. It reminds me of that kid's toy, Night Bright. All the colors are illuminated against a pitch black backdrop. It is so amazing that I do not want to leave. I decide to take a snippet back with me so I cut off a 12" piece of the 3M magnetic tape on which they record the movies, thinking it will help color my world.

Dreams bring color to our world and help us create Heaven on Earth. Like bats, we fly in the night through our own inner city. Everything we have and will experience has already happened. It is all stored within us on the magnetic tape archives in our minds. Even though time is an illusion, it is one of our greatest gifts because it is within time where we are allowed to experience the choices we make to see, like snow through the ashes, the infinite sea of possibilities, and to learn why we make the choices we do. This helps us understand who we are. It is our way of experiencing God. When we experience life, we experience God.

God The Observer and Master Dreamer

The Magic Carpet Ride

In my dream I am traveling to the date February 1st, 2001. I see my sister Rosa and my aunt Helen walking down a street somewhere in the desert but they do not recognize me nor do they seem to be able to see me. I see writing on the walls that I do not recognize as any language I know. The writing looks more like Chinese or Japanese.

I have my money held tightly in my hand. It is so crumpled it looks like a big piece of soggy green bread. The sun is high in the sky and extremely bright.

Rosa and Helen give me a bag and tell me to go back and sell the contents of the bag. I open the bag to look inside and upon first inspection it looks like marijuana. I take it back to them and tell them I am not going to take pot back with me to sell. They tell me I must repay my debts. I look at the contents a second time but now they have changed. The marijuana has turned into wheat. The bag is filled with wheat ears.

Oh my God...I then have a profound revelation that causes me to become lucid. This bag filled with wheat ears represents my book that I am to distribute to feed and teach God's children. It is the symbol of my wheat penny.

With that revelation, I am swept up on a magic carpet and I hear a voice from the heavens say, "It then came to pass when he gave unto Caesar." As I sit up in awe of all that is happening to me and my new mode of transportation, I perch on the edge of the carpet, dangling my feet in the wind. I learn that I can let go of my worries while in flight. At first, I hold on tight to the edge but as I gain courage from the experience, it becomes a natural part of me.

As we gain speed, I stare at my legs and the scenery below me. My legs suddenly become lifeless, dangling like a rag doll in the wind. I then look at my arms and they too are dangling beside me in the same manner as my legs. As I turn to look back I see my entire body dangling like a coat on a coat rack. A great wind comes and in the blink of an eye, I leave my body completely. I then realize I am not my legs, I am not my arms and I am not my body. I am not any part of the body I have left behind.

I then come to rest in a dark barren place where there are millions of tiny green worms on the ground. They slither along the ground, slowly growing into serpents. Fearing they will bite me, I wish to return home. I allow myself to fly away, to fly back home or wherever God will take me, and I fly and fly on my magic carpet ride.

I finally come to rest. I feel as though I am resting in the hands of God because it is the most comfortable feeling I have ever felt. It feels like fur against my skin. I have been taken to a Garden of Eden. There is a great sense of eternal peace and tranquility in the garden. Amazonian sounds echo all around me.

I am then wrapped in something like a turbine around my head, which at first I think might be a serpent. It feels too good to be true and better than any drug I have ever had. My euphoria is incredible. I think someone might be trying to tempt me. I say to them, "The Lord Jesus Christ is my Savior." I do not want to be tempted with pleasurable things, but it turns out they are not tempting me.

I begin hearing someone's voice reading verses from the Bible. "It then came to pass when he gave unto Caesar."

God then puts something in my hand. I hear a voice from behind me say, "Just slide over, Hun."

Instantly, I woke up with full memory of the dream. I had an incredible sense of joy and bliss knowing that God was with me and that I was riding in God's hands. How could I go wrong with God in support of me? It was a dream that validated the work I was doing by following my dream to write this book.

We all have debts to pay but I cannot think of a better way to pay my debts than by doing something that I truly believe in. My purpose is to get people to seriously consider practicing their own religion and to use dreams as a path of illumination. Dreams have the power to produce a spiritual high that comes from living life in the awareness of Christ Consciousness. I am still an addict, except now my drug of choice comes from the dream space and the euphoria that comes from learning how to harness it. Once one has experienced the euphoria and ecstasy of which I am writing, one will seek it endlessly not wanting to live apart from it. I am enflamed by my love for God.

The Eye and Belly of God

As I began my meditation, I had a vision where I found myself in the heavens. Angels were descending to greet me. As they began to descend, the vision became crystal clear and all doubt and fear were lifted.

Yes, it was true; the police officers with veiled faces who had haunted me were not police at all. The caps I thought they had worn upon their heads were not police caps at all; they were halos, and the machine guns they carried upon their shoulders were not machine guns but angelic wings. The policemen were angels sent by God all along to watch over me and secure my safe return.

The number of angels that are assigned to each individual is unfathomable. All of these angels were gathered here for me.

In the Course of a Dream Emanuel for Love

They took me to see a very old bearded man who sat in a violet colored chair made of clouds. The man sat there with a toothpick in one hand, attempting to remove something from in-between his teeth as he gazed upon the heavens. I instantly knew that the old man was me and apparently I had not yet lost my obsession with oral hygiene. I guess I will be forever flossing and picking between my teeth.

As the man sat there with his wooden plaque remover in mouth, he looked up and his thoughts appeared above his head in poetic text. The text scrolled into page upon page and I knew that at *"The End"* he had been written *"A New Dawn."*

I relaxed in my bed, thinking how incredible The Dream is. Looking up, I then beheld in a vision the profile of my Creator in Heaven. I could see His right eye as big as day. I saw the Light of Spirit reflecting upon the perfectly polished lens of His eye; this mystical eye with which He sees all. I was captivated by the light when, in the twinkling of an eye, He blinked. He blinked and I knew then that this was in fact my Heavenly Father. With every thought from His eyes came streams of light. His eyes were like a breath. I then beheld His full and supple lips and the many tiny creases therein. I saw Him inhale, and with the exhale the ethers were ablaze with the blue Light of Spirit.

I wanted to see all of the man whom I recognized now to be my Heavenly Father. I panned back and as He drifted away I saw that He too laid snuggly in His bed. Where His arms met His ethereal sheets, light was transferred from His being to mine and to all of his Creation through the sheets in which he lay. His sheets were the Fabric of Life. In His full and round belly was a large eye. In that eye He held within Him all of Creation while He dreamed the dream we call life.

GOD THE OBSERVER AND MASTER DREAMER

The amazing thing is, I do not make this stuff up. I just describe it the way I see it. It speaks for itself. I know it is what it is because it is too great a thing for me to create without God's inspiration. My love for God is what inspires me and it is the only thing I live for. He is the Master Dreamer. I want to do as my Father does and be a dreamer. What I know is that everything begins with a dream. We can change our world by simply dreaming of a better place and holding on to that dream.

A Visit with Santa Claus

I am in a Harry Potter stadium where I am trying to find my way back home. I go flying and flying on my magic carpet, trying to find my resting place. The people who live in this area travel on bicycles that fly through the air. They simply fly. I feel like I am on Crown Hill where I used to live as a kid. I try to go back to my childhood house but the scenery and hillsides look different. I am slightly disoriented. I land my magic carpet on a hillside and walk along the front yard of a house, not knowing where I am or how to get home. It is about four in the morning, and it is still dark outside. The man of the house is standing near an arched trellis with his two dogs. I tell him that I am lost and disoriented. I ask him if he could please show me the way out and point me in the direction of my birthplace.

He takes my hand under his arm and walks me under the archway and through a door. He opens the door and walks me across the threshold to the other side and says, "There you are." Looking around there is nothing but a dense fog and clouds. Fearing he might leave me here and close the door behind me, I grab tight onto his arm and ask him to please guide me and tell me in which direction I should head. With all the clouds here, I would never be able to find my way back home. He then says, "You can go this way or you can go that way," as he points in opposite directions. Unsatisfied with his answer, I cling to his arm. He then says, "My son, no matter where you go, you pull the universe with you. You are home."

In the Course of a Dream Emanuel for Love

As he says those last three words, his face begins to transform before my eyes. In his face is the face of every human being that has ever lived. With that, I realize who this man is and I become lucid. This is the Face of God. Knowing I need to take in the fullness of this moment, I pause in thought to stare at the fullness with which he holds humanity in his countenance. He now has the look of Santa Claus, with spongy curly white hair, a white beard and rosy red cheeks. He is talking to me and I can see his lips move with his every word.

I began to wake up, and as I awakened and my eyes began to open in real life, I could see this man standing at my bedside. Now fully awake in the presence of Santa Claus, I could hear him saying something. I quickly reached for my voice recorder so as not to miss any words that he might say. I began to lose the signal, so I meditated as he patiently waited for me to ready my recorder and continue the dictation. "Spirituality is a treasure to live for all humanity, to overcome a notion, to be heard in a time when spirits rejoice."

He then began signaling me to come follow him. I was not sure where he wanted me to go because he was standing in front of my closet door. So I said, "Okay, but first I've got to go to the bathroom, would you please wait here and I'll be right back, then we can go wherever you would like me to walk with you."

I got up out of bed and made a mental note of the time. It was exactly 4:33 am on the digital clock in my bedroom. I went to the bathroom to do my business and came back to bed where the grey-haired Santa Claus was still patiently waiting for my return. I hopped back into bed with my voice recorder in hand ready to dictate whatever the old gentleman had to say. He was telling me how to find my way home. He said it didn't really matter which direction you go, you pull the universe with you. He then pulled out one of those birthday party whistles, the type that unravels when you blow air through it. He said it has to do with "zero point" and the sound of the universe when you blow through the party whistle. Each time he blew through the whistle the tube unraveled. I could see a bright red light at the end of it. From blowing his whistle, my bedroom began to fill with red light. The red light emanated from the tip of the extended party whistle.

I gazed into it and saw a crystal lens much like the one I see when I meditate on my third eye. He was basically telling me that he is the force that provides the propulsion energy flowing through the party whistle.

I think they were celebrating my arrival because he continued to blow through his party whistle over and over again. Maybe they knew I was having a birthday party tonight.

His image slowly faded but in the red light that still filled my room I saw a vision of a little cartoon mole or chipmunk that had come to lead me down the road. This creature was telling me to follow him. At the end of the road, I could see a baby chick that had just hatched out of its egg. In the sky was a bright orange sun and in the Heavens I could see a book whose pages were being blown by the wind. The scene reminded me of the California Raisin commercials. In the background, I could hear the words to that John Denver song, *"Take Me Home, Country Roads."*

> *"Almost heaven, West Virginia,*
>
> *Blue Ridge Mountains, Shenandoah River.*
>
> *Life is old there, older than the trees,*
>
> *Younger than the mountains, blowing like a breeze.*

IN THE COURSE OF A DREAM EMANUEL FOR LOVE

Country road, take me home

To the place I belong,

West Virginia, mountain momma,

Take me home, country road.[1[*"*

I am in complete and utter awe, or should I say utter aum, when I read my own dreams. Aum is said to be the sound of the universe. I believe I have seen the face of God and have held his arm and asked him to guide me home. In writing my dream and vision this morning of the grey-haired man that reminded me of Santa Claus, it all resonated within me. At some level I felt God and the Universe were celebrating my birthday with me. Curiously, when I was writing my dream this morning and got to the part that reminded me of the California Raisins, my phone rang once and stopped. I paused for a second to see if caller ID would tell me who was calling but it did not ring again. The phone rang just once and stopped. It was not even long enough for caller ID to register.

I felt a wave of synchronicity flow though me and thought how peculiar. I then remembered back to the dream where Jennifer had given me a cell phone that had programmed in it her number. She had instructed me to use it anytime I needed her. Was this an encoded message from the universe?

Have you ever told a person, "If you want me to pick up the phone, send me a signal by letting the phone ring once, then hang up and wait a second and then call back and I'll know it's you calling me?"

I resumed writing down my dream and as my pinky finger hit the final 'a' in the word California, the phone rang again. I paused to look over at the

---

[1] *"Take Me Home, Country Roads,"* John Denver, Bill Danoff and Taffy Nivert 1971

caller ID. Believe it or not it was an out-of-state call. The display on the caller ID read, "California." A mere coincidence to some, but for me it was my confirmation, which the universe always provides to let me know that I am on the right track and can trust in the messages from spirit that I am receiving. God is so incredibly wonderful. I love God with all my heart, mind and soul.

Eyes On Us – You Are Simply Humanable

I had a dream about three transvestites who are going against all odds with their dreams of being stage performers. To practice their craft, they sing at local karaoke bars in the hopes of landing work or being discovered. This day the lead singer sends the other two out to work one of the karaoke bars in the downtown area while she stays behind to manage their affairs.

It is just before noon and the bar is relatively empty. They are on stage practicing. The one on the right is extremely slender and tall, wearing a blend of blue, white and black. Her hair is jet black and she towers over the other girl, who is a short blond wearing a white and yellow outfit. The bar has floor to ceiling windows that look out onto the street. You can see and hear the performers as you walk down the street. This is how the bar attracts business.

This day the two are singing the Joe Cocker song, "You Are So Beautiful". A major talent agent walking by catches them performing their song on stage and stops into the bar to listen. He likes them so much he offers to do a movie about their life struggle to the top. All over the city their faces are up on billboards. The billboards read: "You Are So Beautiful; Simply Humanable."

My former partner Joe is now dating one of the two girls and they are living together. I call up to Joe's apartment to congratulate him on his recent success and the transvestite he is dating answers the phone. I think to myself, "Wow, she made herself at home with him pretty quick."

IN THE COURSE OF A DREAM EMANUEL FOR LOVE

They invite me over to visit with them. When I get there, I notice there is only one unisex bathroom in the whole building and it is not very private at all. Everyone can see everything you are doing. I am forced to lose my inhibitions because I have to go "number 2" badly. The bathroom does have a folding door that you prop up in front of you to create the illusion that you are sitting in a private stall. They tell me privacy is just a state of mind. The folding door just helps to create the illusion of privacy. In reality, you are wide open from behind and on both sides.

A journalist comes by who wants to do an interview for a magazine. Joe's partner is upstairs getting ready. I am sitting with the journalist on one side of a glass partition. I see his transsexual lover come down and from behind the interviewer, she motions to me, "Do I look okay?" The outfit she is wearing looks fabulous but the shoes do not match. I look at her and with my eyes give her the signal, "The shoes, honey, the shoes." She looks down at the soles of her shoes and gets the message. She runs back upstairs to put on another pair of shoes. She comes back down a few minutes later wearing a pair of night bright shoes. To perfection, she is Simply Humanable.

Some dreams are simply meant to be felt in your heart and carried with you throughout the day. There is nothing we can hide from the universe. We are an open book. We are dichotomies.

The Eskimo Within

Last night as I was falling asleep I had a vision in which I was floating at night over a rural part of town where I could barely see the street below me. I then saw a blue light in the distance and floated over to where the light was coming from. It was coming from the window of a house as if someone inside were watching a very bright television. I was drawn by the intensity and color of the blue light.

With a mere thought, I entered through the window of the house and into the room. I hovered over the light and realized the magnificent blue light was not coming from a television. I suddenly had the feeling that someone above me was shining a bright blue spotlight on the object that I was trying to look at. It felt as if I were hovering under a helicopter searchlight.

As the light from above me illuminated the object I was looking at, I decided to take advantage of this spotlight and come in for a closer look. The combination of the searchlight above me and the light emanating from the object I was trying to look at reflected upon each other, resulting in an incredibly intense light. Yet, I still could not make out what it was that I was looking at. The color of the light was similar in color to the blue flame on a gas burner. I looked carefully at the object trying to figure out what it was. As I came in even closer, I realized I was looking at myself. I was that bright blue object. I was lying curled up in bed in a fetal position. I was shocked and amazed. How could I be looking at me and more importantly, how in the world was I completely aglow in this magnificent blue light? I wanted to know the source of this magnificent light.

I then turned around to figure out where the light from above was coming. I turned and saw a man wearing a thick heavy fur-lined hooded coat. The man was hunched over, trying to look at something in front of him. I could see the fur around the edge of his thick hooded jacket. He looked like an Eskimo in the arctic. He was bent over slightly and looking directly at me. From the expression on his face, I could tell that he had seen something he had not been expecting to see. I almost felt that he had somehow seen me and was wondering where on earth I had come from? I could see him talking to someone in another part of the room he was in.

A woman entered the picture and she too became intrigued with what the Eskimo-like man was looking at (namely me). I must have had a moment of clarity because I was suddenly able to see the Eskimo man and the woman in full color instead of a bluish gray-scale image. I was also suddenly able to hear what the Eskimo man was saying. I could hear his voice and understood what he was saying. He was talking about me. He was asking the same questions I had asked when I saw myself sleeping in bed. He too was puzzled how he was able to see me.

At that moment, I thought, "There is no way I can ever forget this experience," so I did not bother to reach for my voice recorder. Instead I just stayed there to take it all in.

The image then faded and I could no longer hear what was being said, I could only see this man's lips moving. He then walked out of the room and I reached over and grabbed my voice recorder.

When I got to work the next morning, I decided to meditate a bit and see if I could remember what else the Eskimo man had said. I meditated and asked to see him and talk with him that I might know the meaning of his interest in my life. As I meditated, I saw in my mind the eye of my soul. I became aware that I stood in the pupil of the eye; it was like a doorway. I saw several orbs (eyes). Each orb was followed sequentially by another orb or eye, and through the pupil of each orb (eye), I traveled through its connecting pupil, its center core. I could clearly see the iris and pupil of each orb suspended in space. It was like traveling through the galaxies. The orbs were connected like a long string of pearls. I suddenly realized this is what makes up what is termed the silver cord. Each orb was emitting its blue light of spirit. The blue light pulsated through the string of pearls with sacred precision.

I suddenly gained perspective on the orbs and saw the image of a man. He was standing in front of me. I could see right through his mid-section. It was like looking through a viewfinder. As he approached, he began to undo his shirt to expose his belly. In his belly was a circular void through which I could see our universe spinning. I then saw myself approach him and kneel before him. I took my hand and reached into his belly. The core wall of his belly was completely aglow. I then looked inside and amongst the many points of light within him, I found the eye of my soul, the eye of soul that corresponds to my unique essence.

I then saw the profile of my eye and as I did, my eye opened and began to blink rapidly as if it had just awoken from a long night's sleep. I could see the polished glass surface of the lens of my eye of soul and it reminded me of a crystal ball. Deep within my eye of soul, I could see the iris of my eye ablaze with the radiant blue light of the Christ Consciousness.

I looked into the pupil of the eye and there, upon a blue bed of fog, stood a solitary man in the distance. I had a sense that this man, possibly the Christ within me, had been left here waiting for a very long time. I saw him throw his arms up into the air as if to say, "How long must I wait?"

The ethers then came together to create a lounge chair that appeared behind him. The man turned and sat slumped in the chair with his legs outstretched. The fog went dim as night fell once again upon the man.

I was so moved, incredibly moved in my spirit, that I did not need to ponder any more what had been brought to my consciousness, for I had found the Christ within me. How long had he been there waiting for me?

I dropped to my knees in silent prayer, thanking him for waiting so patiently. How could I have let this man sit there alone waiting?

I also realized that he continues to wait in the temples of our hearts, for his children to come home. I can only imagine the feeling of abandonment and desperation of not being able to reunite with his loved one(s). How could I not help this man awaken his children, my brothers and sisters, to the Christ within each and every one of us, that we may once again be reunited as one family in total and complete awareness of our one true essence?

It was the Buddha who said that he had to reject nirvana until every blade of grass was enlightened. How do you convey the Light of God in words and do it justice? There are no words to describe the magnificence that is the Light of God. It burns so passionately in my heart that I cannot contain myself. I am overflowing in rapture and I wish to share it with all of humanity. Please listen to the dream for it holds the Promised Land.

Inter-Dimensional Living

I Hold Your Hand in the Name of Love

I have had many incredible dreams but this one was among my most profound experiences. This had to be what is referred to as astral projection.

In this dream, I find myself wandering around the astral plane communing with other spirits. I recognize I am astral projecting when someone asks me in the dream what time I am going to work. Here the dream is asking me the question I normally ask myself to test and trigger a lucid dream state. I look at my wrist and notice I do not have my watch on. I never take my watch off for any reason, not even to shower. Yet the missing watch is not what catches my attention. It is seeing my hand made not of flesh and blood, but instead, etheric, luminescent and transparent. I am true blue in spirit. Yet without a watch, I somehow know the time is 5 am.

Since it is early and I am not feeling tired, I hang around with friends and show them my new-found abilities of flight. We are all hanging out in one of the rooms of my house. The room has very high ceilings and I can ascend within the room with merely a thought and look down over my friends below me. I can see them turning their heads and following me with their eyes as I fly around the room. The white robe I wear elongates as I ascend and become one with the walls of the room.

I am having so much fun showing my friends, I feel like a child with a new toy at Christmas time. I feel as if I have just graduated to a new level of awareness. As one of my graduation presents, I am given an extremely large red and blue kite. This kite is so large that I cannot keep it in my house. My friends then suggest we take the kite to the building where I work. I am in awe of this kite, which has wings like a bird. The experience is exhilarating. Upon entering the building where I work, I see that there is a large atrium which is three stories tall. This atrium is a perfect place to hang my kite. My friends tell me I can put my kite anywhere I want including suspending it from the atrium ceiling.

"Why would they allow me to hang my kite in this building?" I ask.

"Because it is your building," they tell me.

"My building? What do you mean, my building?" I reply.

"It is your building and it has your name on it. This building was named after you in recognition of all that you have done," they say.

I cannot believe I have a building named after me. I then give instructions for them to hang the kite in the atrium of the building, suspended from the ceiling.

After all this time has passed, someone asks me, "Aren't you going to be late for work?" Again, I look at my wrist. This time my awareness has grown and I realize I not only have an etheric hand, I also have an illuminated body. Still without a watch, I somehow know the time has not changed. It is still 5 am.

"What's up with the time here? How is it I know the time and why is it that the time has not changed? It's impossible for me to be late for work," I gather.

I then go back home and find that my best friend Quetta is sitting on my couch waiting for me to arrive. I have not seen Quetta in ages. I get all caught up in the moment, talking to him as though no time had passed since we last talked. I sit on the couch across from him intent on listening to him talk to me. I then have a flashback to 10 years prior to the day of his funeral when Quetta was laid to rest. He passed away from AIDS. I then realize this is a spirit Quetta and not a physical Quetta.

Fully lucid, knowing this dream moment would slip past me as soon as the dream was over, I knew I had to hold on to this precious moment in time.

Interrupting him, I blurt out, "I LOVE YOU QUETTA! I LOVE YOU, I LOVE YOU SO MUCH."

INTER-DIMENSIONAL LIVING

I cannot stop looking at him and telling him how much I love and miss him.

"I LOVE YOU!!"

He smiles at me with a knowing look on his face. He understands that I know how special this moment in time is. I keep repeating the words like a broken record unable to take my eyes off him until slowly his image begins to fade.

As his image faded, I woke up in real life, thinking, "I made it, I finally made it to the other side and my best friend in the whole wide world. Daniel, whom I had nicknamed Quetta, was there. I then understood it was not Quetta that had faded away, it was me who faded and returned to my waking life as I awoke from the dream.

"But wait, what's this?" Fully awake, I realized I was still holding on to something. I had held on so tight in the dream, I could still feel under my covers something clutched in my hand. I had a grip on something. I thought this might be Quetta whom I was holding on to. I continued to hold on tight, not knowing what to do. I could unmistakably feel the pressure of someone's hand locked in mine. I was holding on to someone's hand, but who's? For the life of me, I was not going to let go. With quick thinking and a quick move, I grabbed the person's forearm with my other hand, determined to hold on. Under my sheets, I could now feel his forearm in my left hand. Whose arm was this?

The sun was just beginning to come up so I could clearly see around my room. There was no one in front of me. I could see no one in my room, not even in spirit form, which I often do see. I continued holding on tight to this person's hand and forearm. Quick thinking told me to feel my way around. I began to run my left hand along his arm. This person's arm was hairless and completely smooth. My left hand reached the outside of his hand. I had both my hands wrapped around his right hand. I could feel his hand and his fingers. Something was different about this hand. It was unlike any human hand. I could feel it as real as anything in real life and there was no mistaking I was fully awake.

Feeling my way around, I noticed the hand was larger in size than any human hand. My hand felt like the small hand of an infant held tightly by his father's hand.

OH MY GOD, I knew whose hand this was. I was holding the hand of GOD! This was the hand of GOD! Yet God remained invisible before my eyes. My eyes were literally bulging out of their sockets and my heart was racing.

I carefully looked around the room when suddenly, from around an invisible presence before me, poked Quetta's head in spirit. There was someone standing between me and Quetta. Someone invisible whose hand I was holding on to for dear life. Peaking around him, Quetta motioned to me like kids do to pull the invisible presence toward me. I knew this was my chance to see GOD with my own eyes. This was my chance to see the face of my Lord and I was determined to do just that. My right hand quickly reached out and grabbed his triceps and I pulled him forward with all my strength.

From behind a veil in front of me emerged the face of a five year old boy with curly glistening blond hair, just like the curls I had when I was five years old. As always, God was full of surprises. Not what I had expected, I decided then to pull the child in closer for a better look. "Who is this child that looks like me?" I wondered.

Looking into his eyes I realized this child was me. This child was none other than me at age five. I am God and God is me, we are one. My heart literally skipped a beat. In shock, I let go of my grip and fell back into my pillow.

I sat up in bed with my eyes wide open, thinking about what had just happened. I then heard the front door open and the house alarm go off. My roommate had just walked in from a late night out. I turned to look at the clock on my nightstand and it was exactly 5 am.

It was one of the most incredible dream experiences I have ever had. It was such an honor and a privilege to see my beloved best friend Daniel, whom I had affectionately named Quetta when growing up. We were and still are inseparable. Our spirits do in fact transcend physical death. True Love is what binds us together.

God is within me. If only for the purpose of reconnecting with our inner child, dreams are worth cultivating. To do so, automatically brings with them all of the benefits that lie just below the surface of the dream world.

Walk With Me - The Bridge to "The View"

I had a dream where I am at the filming of "The View" with Barbara Walters and Joy Behar. Their guest on the show is Oprah. At the commercial break Oprah gets up and walks off stage to make a phone call. I am told that she will not be returning to the stage because she is done with her guest appearance. I think now is my chance to go over and introduce myself and talk to Oprah about my book. She could be interested in reading it and might be able to help me get my message out. I walk around the stage to a reception area but she is no longer there, yet I can still hear her voice in conversation on the telephone.

I see a long blue corridor that leads to the sound room where others are monitoring everything that is happening on the sound stage. Thinking she must be in that room, I walk down the long blue corridor and into the room at the end. She is on the phone talking while at the same time watching what is happening on stage. I quietly motion to her that she should lower her voice because they can hear her phone conversation on stage. She gives me a funny look and points to the stage and asks, "You mean they can hear me over there?" I reply, "Yes, when I was over there I could hear your phone conversation."

As I am telling her this, her face begins to transform before my eyes. She is now white in spirit with glistening golden hair. She then turns and tells me that she is going to go over there and do something about it. She then turns while in spirit and walks through the wall. As she walks to the other side, the floor where she is begins to rise such that now I am in view of the stage and they are in observation of me.

As I look up at my observers, Barbara Walters, Joy Behar and Oprah, I realize Oprah has transformed into my guardian angel Jennifer, and Joy Behar has transformed herself into my spirit guide Felicity. I realize they have been orchestrating this whole event to get me here. Jennifer grabs some silver angelic glitter and throws it down to me. The glitter goes everywhere. My life is now enchanted with this magical angelic glitter.

As I awoke in complete amazement, I quickly grabbed my voice recorder to record the details of the dream. As soon as I was done, I quickly closed my eyes again and began my meditation, hoping to go back. I then started to remember the details of Oprah's phone conversation that I had overheard. It somehow had to do with completing my book. It needed to be finished because time was running out and I had to prepare for my final exam. Somehow this book constitutes the take-home essay portion of the final exam.

Suddenly I fall into a dream state while fully awake, where I report to the classroom on the last day for the final exam. I walk in to the class and the professor hands me the exam and tells me I have until the end of the day to complete it along with submitting my completed book. Since I have time, I decide to take the exam home with me and retrieve my completed manuscript.

INTER-DIMENSIONAL LIVING

Now at my house, I pull out the exam to complete it and set it down on the kitchen table. I open to the first page of the exam and notice there is only one essay question on the entire exam. I am thinking, "How could this be the exam? The essay question isn't even a question."

The exam simply reads: "WALK WITH ME." Knowing my book somehow needs to fully address this question, I sit there completely baffled and unprepared for such a turn of events. As I am staring at the page, void of thought, the page suddenly becomes an orb with the words "WALK WITH ME" suspended in it. The letters begin to get fuzzy. To make things worse, I do not even have my glasses. I cannot afford not to be able to focus on the exam question.

The letters begin to get smaller and smaller to the point where I am afraid they might vanish from within the orb and I will lose my chance to provide an answer to the question.

Refusing to let go of the exam, I remember that I have used the power of thought within dreams before to manipulate the dream. With a focused thought, I will the words to return to the surface where I can clearly see them. I am determined not to lose sight of my exam question. The words obey my thought and return to the surface of the orb but this time they look different. Somehow the phrase reads the same both backwards and forwards. The phrase "WALK WITH ME" is now an ambigram within the orb. No matter how you look at it, it reads "WALK WITH ME."

I am extremely puzzled and cannot figure it out quickly enough. I am worried that I might lose the ambigram all together. I decide to take a chance and reach into the orb with my hand to pull the ambigram out from within the orb. With a weird popping sensation, I succeed at pulling the ambigram from out of the orb. With the ambigram firmly in my grasp, I open my hands but what is in my hand is now an eye. In shock, I drop the eye and awaken.

This dream occurred several months after the previous dream. When I become in tune with my personal dream symbols I experience an incredible sense of inner knowing. I am the ambigram within the orb that is my 3rd

dimensional reality. To become one with our higher selves, our Christ Consciousness, we must be able to walk in full awareness, where we literally become the ambigram.

In some mysterious way when I awoke from the previous dream with the sensation of holding God's incredibly large and invisible hand, I was in fact feeling my own hand from this dream, this future me, where I reached back into the 3rd dimension and plucked myself out. In this dream I stepped into the awareness of my Higher Self and thereby was able to travel outside the 3rd dimension, where I looked back upon my earthy existence to pull my symbol, my ambigram, out from this 3rd dimensional world. To walk with me is to walk with the presence of God and live the Dream.

We are individually responsible for our own spiritual progress and ultimately our awakening. Only you can pull yourself out to trigger the awakening. Those illuminated masters who came before us show us the way and serve as examples for us to follow. Illumination is a task that must be realized from the inside-out. It is with a passion for truth and wanting to know God that you come to know thy own self. I am one with God. I am the five-year-old who accidentally stumbled upon himself and in so doing came to know, understand and experience the oneness of God. Individually and collectively we are the essence and manifestation of the Divine. There is nothing that exists that is not God. All evil is merely a temporary illusion. It only exists as long as we choose to hold on to it. It is real because we believe it to be. That is how powerful our capacity to create is. Yet nothing that is not born of Love is everlasting. Evil will dissolve and fade as mankind slowly awakens.

We live out our physical lives on the sound stage born of the vibration of God's Word. Everything we do is monitored in the name of Love by our

INTER-DIMENSIONAL LIVING

guardian angels, faeries, guides, ascended masters and other celestial being in the higher dimensional frequencies beyond the astral plane. There is nothing we can hide.

Don't Bump Your Head on That Invisible Wall

On this morning, I woke up and let the dogs out to do their business. When they were done, something inside me said, "You're not done dreaming." So I went back upstairs and crawled into bed with the dogs and began my meditation. I never fell back to sleep. What did follow was an amazing out-of-body experience.

While in meditation, I suddenly entered the dream state while fully awake. As if to introduce the characters, I saw a golden skinned man with the head of a lizard standing on the left and facing toward my right. His image slowly faded and I then saw a golden skinned woman who appeared with an unusually round instead an oval face that reminded me of Joyce Jetson. Her image also faded slowly.

I then had a false awakening where I was seeing my bedroom, except that I knew what I was seeing was not my real surroundings because I knew I had just begun meditating and my eyes were closed. I thought this could possibly lead to an out-of-body experience, so I decided to try and pull my consciousness away from where I was lying in bed.

As my consciousness drifted to my right, I saw myself leaving my body. As my physical body came into view, I noticed instead of being on my back meditating, I (this version of me) was on my stomach with my head where my feet should have been. Although I somehow knew it was me, this person was much younger and better looking. Surprised, I wanted to get a better look at the youthful face I wore. I decided to sit up straight. As I sat up, somehow my etheric head hit an invisible wall. For a brief moment, I became disoriented and confused. How is it possible that I felt my head hit the wall? For a moment, I had doubts about whether I was really dreaming or not, but if I was really awake then who was this person lying on my bed beside me?

I decided to try sitting up again but in that moment a bull dog came running into the room barking. I do not have a bull dog so I knew the bull dog and the wall had to be some blockage within my psyche. I refused to be held down or intimidated by this bull dog, or be prevented from looking around by an invisible wall. With determination and conviction, I got up again but this time there was no wall. As I stood up, the bull dog then became more aggressive, pressing his snarling face right into mine. I was not going to be intimidated so I moved forward into the dog and my consciousness entered into the gaping jaws of this ferocious dog. I could see nothing but red vicious anger bubbling up in the throat of the dog. Once inside the belly of the dog, a group of men quickly came to pin me back down to my bed. For a moment, I did not know what to do or think. I was totally unprepared for this turn of events.

I remained calm. Eventually, I said, "Enough is enough. I'm taking back this space." As I said that, everything began to dematerialize and the men who had pinned me down to my bed began to beg and plead with me not to take their space away. I refused their request. I told them the space they inhabited was coming back to me and I was going to heal it and release it back into the universe. The space and the men were drawn into my body. As I exhaled, my consciousness took off in flight and a beautiful pristine ocean appeared. My consciousness flew and soared among the heavens. I flew along a coast line with white sandy beaches.

I then came to a desert with many mounds of dirt that looked like little adobe huts. This was possibly somewhere in the Middle East or some distant planet like Mars. I could see jeeps speeding along the desert in pursuit of me. My consciousness continued to soar. They then called in some helicopters to pursue me, but as the choppers came in closer I realized they were not choppers. They were white flying spirits, like angels. They finally caught up to me and took me upon their wings and we ascended even higher. We finally came to a place where we stopped to rest. They all looked at each other and at me and one turned and looked at another and said, "He has finally arrived."

In my experience, the best time of the day to have altered states of consciousness is when I first wake up in the morning. Meditating immediately upon awakening is something I highly recommend doing. We must reclaim the space where we have allowed fear and negativity to take up residence within us. We share this space with all we create, so it is important to create only from a place of love. We have such an enormous power to change our lives for the better by actively working the dream space. It is the secret to enlightenment.

Be Reborn and Don't Play With Matches

This was one of those rainy Sunday mornings. I got up because the dogs were fussing and wanting to go out. While they were outside doing their business, I had a little debate in my mind on whether to go to church in the rain or hit the snooze button on my alarm clock. Inside I heard a voice say to me, "Why don't you go to church in Spirit?"

"What a wonderful idea," I thought, knowing exactly what that meant. When the dogs were done, we all headed back upstairs and found our way under the covers.

I laid flat and began my meditation. Before long, I could see my third eye looking back at me and from within the pupil of this eye in the heavens, I could see an array of rainbow colored lights emanating from the black depths of my pupil. I gave myself instructions to go through the pupil of my third eye. Once inside, the orb-like space was filled with video screens, each with a different scene playing.

I then heard a voice say, "Aren't you ready to go yet?" I thought my roommate had walked into my bedroom so I opened my eyes to tell him I was not going to church. Instead, I found standing beside my bed two young faeries; a little boy and a little girl. They were so cute, I reached out to them in spirit and hugged and kissed each one of them. The little boy then said, "Come on in here 'n pick one, what'cha wait'n for, we gotta get go'n."

The little boy did all the talking. He had a cute accent and funny way of stressing his N's. The faeries hopped onto my bed and away we went down this wormhole on what seemed like another magic carpet, or more accurately, enchanted mattress ride traveling at light speed.

When we emerged on the other end of the wormhole, it was a world very different, like none I had ever seen. Quite soon we were spotted by a flock of flying brown rats carrying hand held rocket launchers. I did not know if they were good guys or bad guys until they began firing their rockets. Fortunately for us, they were all misguided and shooting their weapons at our shadows. Unafraid, I flew my enchanted mattress alongside them, believing that if they saw me they would know I was not a threat. They were probably just frightened by my shadow. As I passed their field of vision, I realized the only thing they could see or perceive was my shadow and nothing more. They simply could not see me.

INTER-DIMENSIONAL LIVING

We then climbed in altitude, soaring well above them. As we ascended, I saw below us a blue horse-drawn carriage led by four winged black horses. They came in at an altitude well above the flock of flying brown rats yet below the altitude at which we were flying. In the carriage was a young girl in a blue dress with white lace. As her carriage beneath us passed in the opposite direction, she stood up and turned as her carriage sailed by. Looking back, she glanced up at us and waved her arm. As she waved, I waved back.

She quickly turned her carriage around and ascended toward us until she came and scooped us under and we became one. We climbed higher yet, into another dimension where she took me to someone's house. We walked around the small house. I was so amused that I could see this place with the same awareness and consciousness that I experience in my physical world. Everything was so real to me. I wondered if I had left my old life permanently behind.

Inside the house, we walked around admiring all the knick-knacks on the walls. I asked the young maiden in the blue dress why she had brought us here. She answered, "You live here." I looked around again and it suddenly hit me. I recognized all these things to be mine. I was the one who had decorated this house. These were my things, my knick-knacks. I felt a wave of emotion sweep over my body that made me well up inside.

A man in a white medical lab coat then came in through the front door carrying a very large white dog in his arms. I had the impression he might be a veterinarian. He was accompanied by another man. I asked the young maiden if one of these two men was me. To that she answered, "Can't you tell?" I looked at the men again and as the second man who accompanied the doctor sat down, I recognized him to be an old friend of mine. The man with the lab coat now had his back to me. Although he looked different, I knew he was me.

I somehow suddenly knew everything about this man. I watched him as he performed his work on the dog. He suddenly fell ill from a great pain within his chest. I watched him die. I relived the pain of my death down in the depths of my soul.

I asked, "Why did you bring me here to experience this?"

I then heard the voice of the little faerie boy say to me, "Can't you remember, WALK WITH ME?"

"Yes, I remember," I said.

He then said, "Well, why didn't you walk with me? Did you not understand the message?"

I thought this was a good opportunity for me to play dumb and get some inside information from the faerie boy and hopefully have him explain further the meaning of the ambigram.

I replied, "No, I am not sure if I understand."

He curtly replied, "Stop playing with matches."

Hit with a double conundrum for which I could no longer deny my state of affairs, he then jumped up on my shoulders and pressed the base of his palm into my forehead and said, "Be born again."

I feared he might send me back to do it all over again. I grabbed his arm and said, "NO!" I reached up over my head and pulled him in front of my face by his arm where I could see him and said, "Not without first clearing this karma."

He then said, "You're go'n to have to do some—thin bout this."

With that, I placed the image of Christ in my mind and blessed the faerie boy. His whole being illuminated as the blessing went out from me and touched him. He, along with the others disappeared and I remained there by myself. I somehow understood all the cause and effect regarding this past lifetime and its effect on my present life. I knew this was why I suffered today.

I stared at a blank wall thinking, "I must change my world. I can no longer repeat these cycles." I remembered what the Bible said – "You can move mountains if you have the faith of a mustard seed."

I believe! I cannot give up!

With this belief in my heart and focused intent, I was determined to sit there and stare into the blank wall until a path opened up. As I focused ever more intently, an open window appeared in the wall. On the other side of the window I could see three space ships hovering in the night sky, beaming a message down. I stood up and walked over to the window to get a closer look. I knew this had to be the answer I was searching for.

On the other side of the window was a fire escape. I knew I had to attempt flight once again. Not sure if flight was even possible in this dimension and not knowing if I had been permanently born into this reality, I decided to take a chance. I stepped through the window and onto the fire escape. My last thought to myself was, "You had better not try this back home."

While on the fire escape, I was able to clearly see the message being sent by the space crafts. These aliens were broadcasting a message that was intended for me. They had the words of my ambigram written on the outside of their space crafts like on a blimp. On all three space crafts it read: "WALK WITH ME."

I then noticed each space craft carried a communications port on the belly of the craft. It reminded me of the COM port and video port on the back of a computer. I thought there must be a way to connect to their ports and thereby connect with my ambigram. As I thought about how to connect, a whirlwind came and swept me off and away I went on another enchanted mattress ride in the direction of the space crafts.

Mission Control

On this night, while lying in bed meditating, I saw angel hair and apparent patterns vibrating within the angel hair. The patterns began forming images. I distinctly saw the profile of a woman with short hair. She was sitting at a long boardroom table with television monitors all around, similar to what you would imagine NASA's Mission Control to look like. The woman was talking to her colleagues who sat with her at the table. Every once in a while she would turn to look in my direction. Finally, she turned far enough such that I was directly in her field of vision. Hoping she would see me, I waved at her. She immediately looked surprised and turned to the person beside her to say something as though she had unexpectedly felt my presence.

A minute or so passed and eventually she turned again sufficiently to catch my presence. I waved at her a second time. This time she turned and moved to the side allowing me a full and clear view of everyone seated at the table. There were two others beside her. I waved again and with my fingers gave her a count of the persons in the room. I began with my index finger, followed by my middle finger, followed by my ring finger. I indicated a count of three persons including her. I sensed they were discussing my presence and she was somehow the channel or go-between. She confirmed to the others that I was definitely able to see them because I told her how many people were in the room.

By this time, the day had caught up with me and I was simply too tired to stay awake much longer even though I was very interested in discovering why

INTER-DIMENSIONAL LIVING

I was seeing my "mission control" people. Before rolling over, I asked, "Who are you and why are you here?" I also thanked them and proceeded to roll over on my side to fall asleep. It was a quarter to mid-night. I instantly fell asleep.

A few minutes later, at 12:25am, I had a sudden awakening. The first thing that struck me was, "Why do I constantly wake up around this time?" I had just had the following dream:

In the dream, I have a very strong sense that someone is watching me. I am wondering where in the world they could possibly be watching me from? Where exactly are these people? Where did they place their hidden cameras to monitor my life that I cannot see them?

As I walk around, I see someone's computer screen and on the screen is a web portal with details of my life. They have cataloged my entire life including the names of my parents, and brothers and sisters, with little icons that correspond to each person in my immediate family. I do not know whose computer it is but the website clearly contains my personal biography. It is a very modern website with portal features I have never seen before, like something out of a sci-fi movie of the future. This website acts as a portal into my life. My first thought is, "Where did they get the information to create such a portal? Has my computer been compromised in some way? I feel like my privacy has been violated and I am worried that now they are collecting details on my family."

On the site they have all my family portraits that show the members of my family. I want to know where it is that I can hide from their all-seeing eyes.

I now see an incredibly intense white light that is so bright I can barely look into it. I put my hand in front of my face to block the light. I see the shadow of my hand against the light but not my hand. I move toward the origin of the light and I see that it is originating from under the door. It feels like I am in some kind of hotel room or sleeping quarters. I do not recognize my surroundings. The room is dark.

IN THE COURSE OF A DREAM EMANUEL FOR LOVE

I can clearly see the light's point of origin. It is a square, much like the viewfinder within the lens of a camera. The lens looks black yet there is this incredible white light emanating from it. It reminds me of a time when I pointed my computer cam at the computer screen and the image of the screen went off into infinity with each progressive image becoming smaller than the previous one. In the center of the lens was a clear view of infinity. It is like looking through a black crystal, if such a crystal exists, with light everywhere except at its center where utter stillness and complete void exists.

I don't pretend to understand everything I see in my dreams and visions but one recurring theme is the idea that some future me is trying to go back in time and get my attention to possibly change some course of events. One of those, "If only he had realized...," kind of thing. Or, have I possibly found a way to travel forward in time? I also have an extreme sense that the work I am doing with dreams and my writing will somehow change the course of human history. If someone out there is depending on me, I want to be ever present and aware, to hopefully understand what needs to be done for the greater good of mankind. I do know that as long as I follow my heart and my inner voice I cannot go wrong. Whoever these people are, whether within me or in some outer reaches of our universe, one thing is clear -- they have my highest interests in mind. This I know because they have brought me closer to experiencing my Christ self, the light under the door, the gateway to the infinite.

Your Banner Is Held High but Don't Forget Your Wallet

Last night, I had an intense conversation with my roommate and a friend of his, where I shared my story and affirmed who I am called to be, a Child of the Light. What followed tonight would be an affirmation from the heavens by way of a prophetic dream.

INTER-DIMENSIONAL LIVING

I had a dream where I am staying in a hotel and they are preparing to host a convention. Due to the convention, everyone is issued security access badges that grant access to the hotel complex where the convention is being held. On this morning, I leave out of my hotel room headed to catch my train for work. It is a long walk to the metro.

When I arrive at the metro, I realize I left home with just my wallet. I am completely naked. Standing on the platform, I realize I cannot possibly report to work like this, I have got to head back home and retrieve my clothing and access badge. Frustrated with my predicament, I close my eyes to take a deep breath and accept the situation in which I find myself. Trying to relax and release my anger, I stand there for a few minutes to meditate and calm down. I suddenly fall into a wakefully induced lucid sub-dream state within the dream. I am now having a dream within the dream and I am lucid in both states. Knowing I am not going anywhere, I decide to take advantage of this altered state and see where it takes me. With my dream eyes closed, I begin to have a false awakening within the sub-dream where I find myself on the same train station platform. I open my dream eyes to look for differences between my two inner dimensions that hold this train station. I notice the difference is that in the false awakening within the sub-dream, the people standing on the platform have bird-like characteristics as compared to the regular dream where everyone looks normal. Another thing I notice within the false awakening of the sub-dream is that the bird people have the ability to walk through walls. It is like looking at two dimensions of space / time that are superimposed on one another.

Satisfied that I have an awareness of the difference present in both dimensions, I open my dream eyes and head back to my hotel room to get dressed and recover my access badge. As I am walking back, I turn around for a second glance at the train station platform where I had been standing. As I turn, oddly enough both dimensions are now superimposed one on top of the other without the need for me to close and open my dream eyes. There are people standing on the platform alongside the bird people who are holding up a rather large blue banner with white lettering that reads, "You Forgot Your Wallet." Could the message be for me? My situation is not one of having forgotten my wallet but of only having my wallet. Confused, I decide to continue my trek back to the hotel. As I am walking alongside the hotel building, I can see where they are beginning to secure the perimeter in preparation for the conference. Knowing I do not have my access badge, I am going to have to convince the people monitoring the doors of who I am in order to gain access.

The building has glass windows from floor to ceiling such that you can look into the main lobby area from the street where I am standing. There is a side service entrance. I decide to tap on the glass to see if I can get someone's attention. Looking through the glass, I recognize the people inside as those I have worked with in the past. I am sure they will be able to let me in.

I tap on the glass and signal them to open the door. The man in charge nods his head indicating that it is not possible. He motions to me that I am going to have to walk around the building and enter through the main entrance, which is another four blocks away. To further explain his refusal to assist me, he points to a white bridge that separates the perimeter of the building from the main floor, making it impossible for me to enter through the service entrance without a badge. I do not want to have to walk around the building.

I see my two sisters coming out of the building. I think to ask them to bring my badge and clothes out with them but they do not see me waving at them. Once out on the street, my sister Rosa says she left her badge in her room so she is in the same predicament that I am except she is wearing her clothes. My other sister says she cannot go back inside because she does not know the way there without my guidance. She tells me to use her badge, but I know I cannot gain access using the badge of another person.

We sit down in the garden space just outside the building trying to figure out what to do. As we are talking, my uncle Arthur comes up from behind with his two children and tells me that since I am stuck on this side, why don't I watch his children for him while he attends the conference. He says to me, "I consider you to be the designated driver and nanny for the children."

Now I feel obligated to the care of his children. I stand up and walk over toward the hotel windows to have one last look inside and I accidentally catch my reflection in the window glass. I can see myself naked as a blue jay holding my wallet in my right hand. I look at my face and can see a tear streaming down my cheek. As the tear drips off my cheek and hits the ground everything ripples as if I am looking at my reflection in a pond. In the reflection, I can still see in the distance the train station platform and the people who are holding up what I know now to be a banner whose message is intended for me to read. In the foreground, I can see my sisters and the children in my care who now depend on me.

I woke up in that instant in real life with an incredible sense of awe. Beside my bed, floating in the air, was the image of one of the women who was standing on the train station platform in front of the people holding the blue banner. She smiles at me, cocks her head to her right side, and winks. Her image slowly fades away.

Now truly awake, I grabbed my voice recorder that I always have beside my bed and I quickly recorded all the details of the dream and proceeded to get ready for work. I then left the house to catch my train. When I arrived at the train station the image of the blue banner popped into my head again. "You Forgot Your Wallet." Sure enough, eight blocks later, standing at the train station, I was without my wallet.

The dream turned out to be a prophetic dream, and an opportunity to awaken and Live the Dream. I knew from the dream that I could approach my situation in one of two ways. I could be angry with myself or accept life on its own terms and try to figure out what the universe was trying to teach me. In this precious moment in time I could attempt to look through my physical world and into a multi-dimensional reality that lies just beyond the visible world.

I tried to make the best of my situation and grabbed the book I had been reading from my backpack, heading back home to retrieve my wallet. I had left off on a chapter entitled, "Debriefing Room for the Children of Light from Earth." It described the mission for Light Workers; those who chose to incarnate at this time in history to help bring back divine truth, wisdom and knowledge in an effort to help raise the consciousness of the entire world, thereby awakening the soul of humanity to the higher dimensions of light and love. I had never read the chapter before this day. As I read the words in this chapter of this book, I began to feel a presence and voice coming through the pages. The chapter was speaking directly to me.

It is my identity contained in the wallet, who I am, which I forgot the day I came into this world naked as a blue jay. It is also why I am here -- to find myself and remember my original purpose and mission as a Child of the Light. This dream wallet contains information about who I am. It also holds my spiritual cash and karmic debt, an awareness of my chosen path and purpose, and the role I play in the master plan. Who I am, is the only thing worth having in life. Finding someone's wallet paints a picture of who the person is and provides a means of survival and ticket to ride the train of life on whose tracks we experience time.

It was very cold this morning and from the long walk my nose dripped a droplet of moisture like a teardrop upon the page of the book. I felt a sudden echo and felt the ripple the dream had impressed on my awareness. I continued to read about how so often, as children of the light, we feel alone in the world. We should rest assured that we have many in the heavens at our side continuously in support of us. It said *they hold our banners high* with our names on them to cheer us on along our chosen path.

This dream held a spiritual awakening and an affirmation that I am a Child of the Light and all those who are beside me reading along on this journey are called to be Children of the Light. It is time to awaken for morning has come. We are called to hold the light and help awaken the rest of humanity. The call is out. Awaken, dear Children of the Light. Awaken.

Right Living

You Cannot Change Nature; Just Clip Your Coupons and Read the Articles, Says The Dove

Right living must begin with a good measure of self-acceptance. I cannot live right if I do not feel right within myself about who I am. My whole life has been a struggle to accept who I am and where I am at any given time in my life. Having been given a second chance at life after my near death experience, I felt I had to right every possible wrong I had done. I even questioned if now was the time to try and live a celibate life or try a straight relationship. Because I am an obsessive-compulsive person, I have a strong tendency to take everything to an extreme, which to my advantage did include my spiritual pursuits. I now found myself struggling yet again with my homosexuality.

I had a dream where Jerry, my first partner, could not wait to start dating Joe, my third partner, after we separated.

I feel I did something to deserve it but at this point I have no control over the situation. I do think it is in poor taste for two of my ex's to get together. I know the right thing is to simply step away from the situation and wish them well.

Joe then starts telling me about my old dog Chela who passed away before I ever met Joe. He is trying to tell me that he KNEW Chela was a small dog. I tell Joe that having never met Chela, he is in no position to comment about her size. He responds by saying that he knows it to be true. I tell him, "Just because you say it and you believe it doesn't change the fact that Chela was born a Chow Chow, which does not make her a small dog." I tell him, "She is categorically a large breed of dog. You can't change who she was naturally meant to be."

I leave and find myself in an elementary school. They have called for early dismissal. They want everyone to evacuate the building to have the janitorial staff perform extensive maintenance on the building. I apparently did not know this had been requested. I remain in the building after everyone has left. There are some children roaming the halls who have defied the notice to leave the premises. The janitors and cleaning people are now rolling in and beginning their work. I see one of the maintenance people sitting down and clipping coupons out of a magazine. I suddenly remember I need to buy deodorant. I go over to him and ask him if he has a coupon for deodorant.

"Of course I do", he replies. Without thinking, I take the coupon from him. Feeling a sense of conflict within me, I immediately realize I made a mistake in not asking him if I could have it. I ask him if he has a use for the coupon, to which he says that he intends on buying deodorant.

I hand him back his coupon, playing it off laughingly. I jokingly ask him how much he paid for the magazine because I want to buy one myself to clip the same coupon. He says the magazine costs $2.50.

"That's not a savings," I tell him, "The coupon itself has a value of $2.50 so you are not gaining anything from buying the magazine."

"You're wrong," he says, "There IS something to be gained. You receive the benefit of reading the articles in the magazine."

I awoke suddenly in the middle of the night and as soon as I opened my eyes I heard a voice say to me, "Hi… (pause) How are (nearly inaudible) you?" I remained still to keep from losing my altered state of consciousness and answered within my mind, "I'm good, what are you doing here?"

"Don't you need to go to the bathroom?" I heard the voice say.

"Yes, I do," I replied. I then proceeded to get up to go to the bathroom.

When I was finished, I came back, recorded the details of the dream and once again laid snuggled in my bed, returning to my meditative state.

Immediately, I saw the face of a young man in his 30's. I had never met this guy before. His face was as clear as watching a black and white TV, except the contrast was a bit off such that the black was a pale shade of grey. It was as if the contrast on the tube was out of whack. I noticed that when he spoke, his lips pulled to his left and he did a gnawing motion with his jaw like birds do with their beaks. I could see his mouth moving but I heard no sound. I remained still, receiving his message telepathically. As he neared the conclusion of his message, I noticed that his mouth began to change. I could see the inside of his lower jaw transform to that of the bill of a bird. This man was, "The Dove". His message came signed, sealed and delivered.

There are some things in life that we must simply come to accept regardless of what our own personal beliefs might be. These things are God's alone to know. We all carry our own thorns in our side. Letting go and letting God allows us to move into a space where we can call upon the janitorial staff within our learned minds and rid ourselves of the old notions that no longer serve any purpose for us. We must return to a state of child-like innocence where we can see everything with an open mind, read our magazines and experience life with a sense of adventure. We have the entire Kingdom of Heaven within us waiting to assist in clearing the space for us to receive the new instructions of the Aquarian Age.

You Are At the Crossroads, Trust and Be the Better Man

Last night I had a dream where I am watching a movie I desperately want to see. Unfortunately, the movie is playing at a friend of a friend's house whom I am not close to. I do not want to depend on his hospitality to see the movie. Joe takes me over there and puts the movie in the VCR and tells me that I can watch it in their house. I watch practically the entire movie and as it nears the ending I hear Bruce, who is the owner of the house, getting ready to leave for work. I think he is going to ask me to leave without allowing me to see the ending. I know that if the cards were turned, I probably would not want to leave someone in my house that I did not have a close relationship with. To my surprise, he tells me I can stay and make myself at home.

"Wow, he's a better man than I am and definitely more trusting. What prevents me from being that type of man?" I think to myself.

With that thought, my alarm rang. It was 5:45am and I religiously hit the snooze button and dropped into my meditative state. As soon as I closed my eyes, I had an out-of-body experience of sorts where I found myself hovering over a crossroads. The sun had not yet come up. It was dark out and the street lights were still lit. I could clearly see the sparse traffic traveling the dark country roads in both directions. I tried to figure out if I had ever been at this crossroads before.

I held my altered state, wanting to know what else was here for me to experience. I could see a light blue fog-like haze sweeping across my field of vision from upper left and down toward my lower right in an arc.

My alarm rang a second time. Not quite ready to brace the cold of daybreak, I practiced my religion and hit the snooze button a second time. This time I closed my eyes and saw four moon-struck bears doing what appeared to be a circus act. They were performing summersaults hand in hand, one over the other. I watched them as they played and frolicked together in perfect harmony with each other. My alarm rang again; time to start my day.

How often have I stood at the crossroads and made the choice to do it on my own and not depend on others? I now realize I am part of a collective system, a node on a network of celestial beings here with a common purpose. To become my full potential, I must connect with others and open up to allow myself to channel divine energy.

We are conductors of the divine. When we connect and focus our intent on channeling only the highest vibrational frequencies of love, gratitude, kindness, willingness, openness, sincerity, peace, understanding, compassion, gentleness, and forgiveness, we place ourselves in a space where miracles happen. It helps to step into the observer role of the Higher Self and be fully present in everything we do. In this state of oneness with our Higher Self anything is possible. We are empowered to make manifest our dreams. If we can dream it, in time it will become our reality. This is why mastering the lucid state is so important to taking control of our destiny. Lucid Living is to be firmly seated in the driver's seat.

Be Mindful of Your Responsibilities

Last night I woke up around 5:20am feeling I had to go to the restroom as usual. I then noticed through the corner of my eye a green translucent figure standing about three feet away from my bed. It was a short angelic person about four feet tall. It clearly had the profile of an angel with wings standing about a foot and a half above his or her head. I could not tell if it was a boy or a girl.

In the Course of a Dream Emanuel for Love

I tried to communicate mentally with the young being but I did not get any response. I laid there mesmerized by its beauty. I reached out my hand, hoping my angelic visitor would feel welcome. To my amazement, the little angel reached back and grasped my hand. Its green luminescent light enveloped my palm. I felt the pressure of its firm but gentle grip as it held my hand.

I remained there in a meditative state with my eyes open and firmly fixed on the vision in front of me, not knowing why it had come to pay me a visit. After about five eternal minutes the angelic figure slowly faded without speaking a single word. I then got up, turned the light on and looked around the room to see if any traces of its presence had graced my room. The angelic spirit was completely gone.

I went to the bathroom and then returned to bed. With the light on, I recorded the details of the vision. I then laid back in bed to meditate and fell into a dream.

I am left to take care of a litter of puppies. There are three puppies, one white one and two grey ones. I am feeling very forgetful and absent-minded. I am told that I left the mother dog in the car all day alone by herself. I must have been on autopilot or just not paying attention because I do not remember having been assigned the responsibility of caring for the mother dog. If I had been aware, I have to believe, I would have taken better care of her. I try justifying my actions. I am told someone luckily passed by and let the dog out of the car. The puppies have not had much to eat. It is Christmas time and they are deciding what gifts to hand out to the children.

I am absolutely convinced that my angels and spirit guides are able to influence my dreams by stepping into my aura while I sleep and combining their energy field with mine. This is the Holy Spirit that God promised He would send to teach us all things.

We all suffer from dream forgetfulness. Luckily, we have our guardian angels who come in the night to help us "let the dogs out."

It is up to me to learn to pay attention, become aware of my responsibility and apply what is being taught to my waking life, that I may change and transform my inner and outer world. These lessons are intended for my highest good. Some work happens solely on a subconscious level but as we mature and begin to awaken, we must take the dream experience to the next level before we can break free.

Knowing this, I am compelled to share this knowledge and power of transformation. It is my first and foremost responsibility to humanity. It is the only thing that matters to me in life. The treasures to be found in the dream space have the potential to change us forever. They are earth shattering. To be within this awareness is to behold the second coming of Christ.

Eventually, we must break free from the egg shell of religion that has protected us up to this point in time. We must evolve and learn to practice our own personal inner religion. We were meant to take wings and fly like our angelic cousins and sail the heavenly winds. There is a whole other world to be experienced once we leave our shell behind. No words can ever fully describe the ecstasy and bliss I have experienced traveling these other worlds. It is our birthright to stand up, break free and claim our divinity for ourselves. This physical existence is not all there is to life.

You are Headed in the Wrong Direction -- Meet Us on the Second Floor

I find myself in a building and over the PA system I can hear a call to evacuate the premises. "There is a fire in the building. Please evacuate the building immediately." Hearing this, I go to the elevators and push the call button. The elevator comes and without thinking I get on, but the elevator is headed in the wrong direction. As the elevator doors are closing I see that someone left a sign on the elevator door that says, "Ruben, meet us on the 2nd floor."

Instead of going down, the elevator goes up and stops on the 9th floor. Not knowing what floor the fire is on and having seen the sign alerting me, I panic. I think, "Oh shit! I wasn't paying attention again. I know I should not use the elevator in the event of an emergency."

I breathe calmly, knowing God is with me. The elevator stops on the 9th floor and the doors open. Once again not paying attention, I stay on the elevator. The doors close and the elevator begins its decent to the 2nd floor where it stops and I get off. Everyone is waiting for me. I am safe now.

I learned for my safety to pay better attention to the signs along the road.

To drive the point home, I find myself in a second dream. I am at a relative's house. Their little boy has been getting into a bad habit of over sleeping. I want to help the boy and encourage him to start his day off right. I see the little boy running over to greet me. I stand up and realize I am wearing the young boy's pajamas, which look ridiculous on me. The pajamas stop at my knees. What am I doing wearing this little boy's pajamas?

RIGHT LIVING

I had been struggling with a key decision I needed to make concerning October 12th. I was conflicted among several options regarding the right thing to do. I was tormenting myself, going back and forth, playing out the scenarios in my head. I was mentally tired and alas, I decided I could not torment myself any longer. Before going to bed that night, I thought I had the answer. I had decided to just take an action and not look back. I made the decision and placed the consequences in God's hands. By morning, before I had acted on the option, I knew my decision was not the right one. This showed up glaringly in my dream. I would have been acting according to old patterns of behavior.

I cannot help others unless I learn to help myself. I have come to believe that by calling on God through my dreams I can and will receive an answer that will enable me to make better decisions. How wonderful it is to get a sign from spirit so specific as to say, "You are headed in the wrong direction, meet us on the second floor."

I took the next right step and exercised my 2nd option, knowing God was with me. I felt good that day knowing I had made the right decision, which freed me to enjoy the blessings God had waiting for me that day and every day.

Dear Abby, I have a Lint Problem

I had a dream in which I had accept considerable financial help from my friend Abby. Now I do not know whether I should pay it back in some way or accept it as having been a gift of good will. Should I take inventory of acts of kindness? A part of me does not want to pay it back. I am a generous person and I give of myself in other ways. I should not have to pay her back, but I feel I owe her a debt of gratitude.

I see someone's shadow under my bedroom door and my gut tells me it is Abby. I open the door and Abby has her back to the door, bent over and obsessed with picking lint up off the floor. I ask her in a very judgmental way, "What are you doing outside my door?" I am insinuating that she is trying to eavesdrop on my closed door conversation with myself. Now I not only feel bad for taking my misdirected frustration with myself out on her, but also for not wanting to pay her back. I cannot hide behind the door anymore because I am sure she overheard me talking to myself about my inner struggle and whether I should pay her back or not. I have no choice now but to face my own demons.

I was my own worst enemy. I was the person I had harmed the most. There came a time when I had to confront my own demons and forgive myself. It was the process through which I learned to love myself. Judge not, not even thy own self, as it only introduces guilt, shame and confusion to the situation. I had to see the obsession with lint for what it was and free myself of it. It is always better to act from a position of Love.

Don't You Remember You Can Fly?

In this dream, I check myself into a hospital overnight to undergo a routine procedure. I am told I will be out by 3pm the following day. During my stay at the hospital, I am allowed to take a dip in their bathing pool to cleanse myself. The pool is so refreshing and nice that I want to take the experience home with me. Even though I know I cannot take it with me, I know I can always come back here for additional treatments. I go back home feeling so good I decide on the spur of a moment to throw a barbeque and invite friends over to share a good time.

Joe has previously committed time to spend with his mother. He is to meet her at 5pm, which conflicts with the little get-together I am planning for myself and my friends. He asks me if I can cut my get-together short and accompany him to meet his mother. For the first time, I am living my purpose and enjoying spending quality time with myself and my friends. I do not want to cut my celebration short. I tell him I cannot go with him. I do not want to limit my celebration. I want to be able to enjoy the experience of having friends over and not feel rushed. He reluctantly agrees to take care of his business with his mother and come back later.

The friends I have over are people I have not seen in many years. They are cherished friends from old. In chatting with them, we share all that we have accomplished. I am told that all of my friends are now commercial pilots, licensed to fly large passenger planes. I am amazed that they have licenses to fly. They take me to the flight training center. The lights are dim in the training center and everyone appears to be very relaxed. A sense of peace and tranquility is everywhere.

One of my friends says to me, "Did you forget that you know how to fly?"

"Know how to fly? Do I have amnesia or something because I really do not remember?" I reply.

"Yes, you know how to fly. You used to always fly those large passenger planes. I'm sure you would remember if you sat in the driver's seat," he says.

Another friend confirms my flying ability and suggests that if I am unsure of myself to try taking one of those mid-sized planes out at night with no passengers. The planes are empty at night and are available for anyone to take out on lessons. If I do, she says, my memory will surely come back to me.

I have never thought I could have the discipline to master such a skill as flying commercial planes, nor do I feel I could take on that level of responsibility. My friend tells me to come back at night and one of the guys in the flight training center will help me become readjusted.

I must be health conscious and partake in a well balanced diet, with proper rest and exercise. I need to cleanse my body of impurities and connect with like minded individuals. These things aid me in creating a light body and improve the recall of my past.

We all suffer from amnesia. It is through harnessing the dream space of our flight training center that we are restored and everything we have worked for in previous lifetimes is returned to us so that we may come back into the fullness of who we were meant to be. We were all born to fly. No one else can do the work for us. Sooner or later the inward journey must be made. No matter what obligations we may have in our lives, we must remain true to our spiritual needs.

Today I have a great sense of purpose, I am free and I can fly.

An Angel Calls – Learning to Color between the Lines

This morning my alarm clock rang and I quickly turned it off and began my meditation, trying hard to remain conscious. While in meditation, I suddenly saw before my mind's eye a white tablet with pastel blue and pink clouds drawn on it. The tablet had inscribed on it a message. I immediately thought this might be a message from God that I needed to be aware of. It was written in a language other than English, similar in script to Aramaic.

Even though I could not read the words, I felt the message in my heart. The message described a child's love for God. It was so touching, tears streamed down my face. After a few minutes meditating on the message, it suddenly hit me that they had used my crayons to color this tablet. I had recently purchased a box of crayons during my last trip to see my parents in California. I had taken my parents shopping at a thrift store and for some odd reason these crayons caught my attention. The child in me wanted the crayons. I bought the crayons and a cute Nemo carrying case and brought them home with me.

When I got home from the trip, I took the crayons and placed them in a wicker basket with a few white cards. I was going to allow my inner child to draw. I then placed them on the floor beside the altar I have in my basement. I figured I would leave them there until I had more time to actually devote to working on the task.

Days went by and I had already completely forgotten about the crayons until this vision. I assumed the vision was now calling on me to allow my inner child the means of expressing himself.

I got up out of bed and ran downstairs, eager to retrieve my crayons. When I went to grab the basket, I noticed something unusual. There was now a single crayon in my offering bowl that I normally fill with water. How did the crayon get there? I never thought to place a crayon in my offering bowl. No one had been in the house to disturb my basket of crayons. Of all places to put it, why was it in my offering bowl? As I studied the mystery of the crayon, in a distant room of the house I heard my cell phone ring once and stop. I knew this had to be a calculated move from a helpful but slightly mischievous angel.

Right living requires that I get in touch with my inner child and work on healing all the wounds that exist in my psyche. I must also return to my innocence and see life though child-like eyes, with the optimism to embrace an endless sea of possibilities. I must allow myself to dream again.

How About Some Crystal Light with that Na Mu Myo Ho Ren Ge Kyo?

Ever since Joe moved out of the house, I have cleaned up after myself religiously. I make it a point to wipe the kitchen counters and rinse off any dirty dishes and stick them in the dishwasher before I retire for the night. The kitchen counters are always spotless. It makes me feel good to come home to a clean house every day. I do this in part because I have to set a good example for my new roommate. I do not want to clean up after anyone other than myself, so the best way to ensure that the house stays clean is to make sure I clean up after myself. Then I'm in a better position to request the same from my roommate in return.

This night, after doing my routine with the kitchen, I locked the house, set the alarm and headed upstairs to retire to my bedroom. I laid in my bed and began my meditation. I immediately had a vision in which I saw my surroundings, yet my eyes were closed. I saw a woman from behind walk down the hallway and turn to walk down the stairs. I thought....now what are they up to? I then heard a noise downstairs and the dogs started to bark. I thought it might be my roommate but I had not heard the front door open and the alarm did not go off. I thought maybe it was my cat Sable, but he was lying next to me purring. I did not feel like getting up out of bed to go investigate so I simply continued my mediation.

I was somewhat tried of repeating my usual mantra sound of OM. I was also tired of OM MANI PADME OM. Not having anything else, I thought maybe I could just make up a new mantra. Those mantra words are as good as made up to me, so I decided to give it a try and jazz it up a bit. I came up with SING YING HING HO. After a few repetitions of my new mantra, I could not contain my laughter. I imagined how silly I must sound in the heavens. I was sure the angels in heaven listening to me were probably chuckling under their breath.

I still could not sleep so I decided to get up and head downstairs for a late night bowl of cereal. I walked into the kitchen and the first thing I noticed was a bottle of my new orange flavored Crystal Light sitting on an immaculately clean kitchen counter. It was a new flavor they had just released, which I had picked up at the grocery store earlier in the week. I am a Crystal Light junkie. I have all the flavors in my cupboard and I love to mix the flavors to create new concoctions.

I was absolutely sure I had left the kitchen counter perfectly clean before heading upstairs. I even remember spraying down the kitchen table and countertops with Windex. My pitcher in the refrigerator was ¾ full so I would not need to brew up a new concoction. The seal on the package was intact and showed no sign of tampering. I knew my roommate had not been home. As a matter of fact, he had not been home in days.

I knew this had to be the work of Spirit, but why would they be calling my attention to this orange and white package of Crystal Light. I studied the package carefully to look for any hidden patterns. I ate my bowl of cereal, retired to my bedroom, popped a sleeping pill and passed out.

In the morning, I had planned on waking up early to go to the gym. When my alarm clock sounded, I inadvertently hit the off button instead of the snooze button. As per my normal routine, I began my meditation. It was a wonderful meditation with yellow and orange moonstruck figures. I became lost in the images and a feeling of timeless bliss. I then thought, "This is going on too long. The alarm clock should have sounded by now."

I looked over at my clock and 30 minutes had already gone by.

"Darn it, too late for the gym," I muttered, so I reset the alarm for another 45 minutes and resumed my meditation.

The yellow and orange colors became a beautiful burning flame the size of a campfire. The yellow flames sat literally at the tip of my nose. The campfire light was displayed in my mind in unrivaled high definition; absolutely crystal clear was this burning flame. I was amazed at how real it looked. I watched the flames rise and fall. I was awestruck. I had no sensation of heat on my outer body, yet a feeling of incredible warmth filled my heart. I somehow knew this was my burning bush, my direct experience with the Holy Spirit within my soul.

My alarm clock finally rang. Feeling totally invigorated, I got up out of bed, let the dogs out and began doing push-ups and curls. In no time at all, I had done the entire workout routine at home that I would normally have done at the gym.

I thought maybe Spirit was trying to tell me that sometimes you have to switch it up a little and vary your routine. Mix it up like you do your Crystal Light. The minute my thought came back to the symbol of the Crystal Light from the night before, my cell phone rang on queue indicating I had a message. "Hmm, could that be a synchronistic message from Spirit?" I thought. My cell phone had been on all night and had not rung. Why now, when the thought of Crystal Light was on my mind? I knew this too was the work of my Spirit guide who pre-programmed my cell phone with her number so that I could call upon her any time I needed her. I knew in my heart it had to have been she who placed the Crystal Light on my counter.

I continued to get ready, left the house and headed for the metro. As I arrived at the metro, I looked up at the morning sky and thought, "What a wonderful way to start my day." At that precise moment in synchronous fashion, I looked down and upon the ground was a shiny penny. Here was another confirmation from Spirit. I had no reason to doubt. I knelt down, gave a quick thank you to Spirit, and picked up the penny.

As I stood back up and lifted my eyes, walking toward me was a short bald Buddhist woman, who could have been a man as she appeared very androgynous. She had a golden bronze complexion that added to her incredible radiance. She was a walking bottle of Crystal Light. She wore the exact same bright colors as the packaging on the Crystal Light; a bright saffron orange robe with a long white scarf around her neck that draped over her chest and down her front to about her thighs. She had a thick rope-like belt tied around her waist that held her robe and shawl in place. Her face was the exact image of the Buddha.

As I passed her on the escalator something inside told me to stop. I turned around and headed back up the down escalator to meet her. I asked her, "What faith are you?"

She said, "I'm a Buddhist."

I told her I was trying to chant last night and wanted to know if she could give me a Buddhist mantra to chant.

She said of course, "Na Mu Myo Ho Ren Ge Kyo."

Knowing I would never remember it, I asked if she could possibly write it down for me. She quickly pulled out a small pad of paper from a knapsack she carried and proceeded to write it down for me while at the same time guiding me in the correct pronunciation. She told me it was from the Lotus Sutra. I told her I knew today was going to be a glorious day. I gave her my blessing and she bowed her head and went on her way.

On the train she sat kitty corner to me. I watched her as she sat silently in meditation. I wanted to go over to her and in gratitude offer her the penny I had found but she was in such a peaceful state I did not want to disturb her. In the seven years I had lived in my neighborhood and ridden the train to work I had never once run across a robed Buddhist. There were simply none in my neighborhood. I knew she had to have been sent by God to deliver a mantra for me to chant. She was my Crystal Light. She was an answer to a prayer.

In the Course of a Dream Emanuel for Love

We really do have to mix things up a little. I appreciate being able to learn how other cultures express their interest and love for God. I have searched earnestly across all religions and when stripped of dogma and ritual, I have found no contradictions. If we can move past the names we have chosen to assign to God, whether in religion or mythology, we find that we are more alike than different. When seen through the universal language of symbols we are all describing the same thing. We are one family, one creation, one body. To limit our experience of God is like never having admired the soles of our feet or the palms of our hands. Let us stop for a moment to caress them and connect with their energy. They tell a story that transcends this lifetime. They hold the imprint of humanity. They speak of who God is and where He has been. They are the beginning and the end. To know them is to know God. God's presence is closer than we think.

The Higher Self

The Satyr of My Life

Last night I had a dream where I am at Michael's house. There are people who want to persecute me because I am the daughter of The Man. I do not know who I can trust. I feel they are manipulating my circumstances to set me up in an unfavorable light. Michael wants me to make love to him. As it turns out, Michael is actually trying to protect me by getting me to say that I love him. It is the admission and confession of my heart that they are looking for from me.

The bad guys are on one side and the good guys are on the other. I feel like I am playing out a scene from the musical, "West Side Story."

I ask my father telepathically, "How do you plan on getting me out of this mess?"

The leader of the bad guys confronts me and asks, "Who is here to protect you?" His thugs are behind him in a show of force.

I do not say anything but I think to myself, "If he only knew the invisible force that supports me he would not be standing in front of me with that attitude."

In that moment in thought, I have a spiritual awakening and it occurs to me that there is nothing to fear if I have God on my side. I state, "There is absolutely nothing to fear!"

At that moment the leader of the bad guys senses that he cannot win. It is the very last minute of the 11th hour. My father comes and whisks me away and takes me to a monastery.

In the Course of a Dream EMANUEL FOR LOVE

As we are in flight, I turn and ask, "Wait a minute, are they going to let me finish writing my book at this monastery?" He tells me that this turn of events is not exactly what I had been expecting. It will however allow me to be of service to Christ.

I think, "As long as I am serving Christ it really does not matter what they have me write about." That is assuming it is still a writing project. I then hear my alarm clock go off with a song being played, "Don't you remember the day when you walked away and left me." I get up to look at the time on my alarm clock but then I remember that my alarm clock does not have a radio. I therefore must still be dreaming.

Now fully lucid, I know I am having a false awakening. I look carefully at the digital alarm clock that sits on my night stand and notice the clock has two times displayed on it as though it has the ability to display multiple time zones. One is displayed in gold numbers and the other, slightly above and to the left, is displayed in white numbers. Just to the right of the white numbers is a red indicator denoting that the alarm had been set at some point in history to go off precisely at this time. It was time to wake up.

I then opened my eyes in real life to grab my voice recorder and record all that I had seen. When I was done, I placed it back on the night stand and closed my eyes and began to meditate. I then saw a moonstruck man get up out of bed and head into the shower. I opened my eyes again in awe of this multi-dimensional awareness and the ability to dream while fully awake. This was too incredible and simply beyond words. I contemplated whether I should grab my voice recorder again but I did not want to lose the transmission.

I closed my eyes and in a vision I saw a very bright blue spinning mandala with a white center. As if struck by a strobe light at varying intervals, I was able to see the mandala in full detail even though it was spinning. The level of detail was far beyond anything I could ever duplicate. I could not pass up the experience. I grabbed my voice recorder to log the details of the vision.

THE HIGHER SELF

I shut my eyes again and immediately returned to the blue, white and black outlined mandala. Then from the horizon began to rise a blue sun. As the sun rose, I realized it was not a sun at all but the top of a man's head and the back of his shoulders as though he had been lying upon a table sleeping. As the moonstruck man lifted his head and shoulders I saw his forehead and eyebrows. He was bald on top with short straggly hair along his temples. He reminded me of Albert Einstein because he had an incredible air of wisdom about him. I wanted to know who this blue man was. A part of me felt like I knew him.

The rest of his face slowly came into view as he lifted his head. He wore a short but thick beard and mustache. I now knew who this man was. He was a 90-year-old me. He had my face. I was beside myself, astonished, wondering if this was what I was going to look like at the age of 90. I could not stop looking at the man. He slowly stood up and I saw his upper torso. His torso and arms were massive like an Olympic gymnast. I was now befuddled.

The man was becoming aware of my presence. As he struggled to make sense of what he was looking at, it suddenly hit him and in shock he took off running at an incredible speed. I called out to him, "Please don't leave." As he ran, my consciousness followed. I then became aware of the man's lower body. He had the lower body of a goat that allowed him to run with the speed of an animal.

I opened my eyes immediately thinking, "What did I do wrong? Have I displeased God? Do I need to tame the beast within me?" This imagery had to be an accurate depiction my subconscious mind served up for me because the image of a Greek Pan was nowhere in my waking consciousness. Though troubling, I had to accept it as who I am today. I looked up the Greek mythological god Pan, the satyr which is half man and half goat, to see what he represents. He was the god of nature who watched over shepherds and their flocks. Was I a Pan, a satyr of some sort?

I was unsettled by the images my subconscious was using in describing me. I thought of positive ways this image might be applied to my life. The next morning on my way to work on the train I was reading, *"Dreams, Your Magic Mirror,"* by Elsie Sechrist. I had left off on Chapter 16, *"The Cross and Other Spiritual Symbols."* In the very first paragraph she says,

> *"From time immemorial, the cross has been symbolic of man's fall from spirit into matter and the need to crucify or control his lower animal nature. Certainly Christianity accepts these implications. The ancient symbol of the cross with the serpent entwined about it depicts man's fall into matter and the necessity for carrying one's own cross in order to be resurrected—lifted up in consciousness."*

There is also the idea that my awakening was preordained to occur at precisely this time in history and not only mine but by extension the awakening of humanity as a whole. This is my purpose -- to help humanity awaken. I am definitely awake and fully aware of my God Self, my Higher Self. As one who has just awoken from a long sleep, my lower body remains in darkness and fear under my sheets. This lower nature now awaits its crucifixion. I must bring it out of its darkness. As my awareness merges back into my Higher Self, a new day is able to dawn. I now have a choice to make. Do I get up out of bed, clean myself up and prepare to face the new dawn, thereby crucifying my lower animal self, or do I lay my head back down and ignore the sound of my internal alarm clock and return to a state of eternal sleep? Today, I choose to awaken.

Life is riddled with irony. Part of the process of waking up is to become aware of the riddles and synchronicities that are happening all around us. The joy is in discovering one's true nature by examining the riddles.

THE HIGHER SELF

Wrapped Around Your Finger

Today as I awoke I came to understand the purpose of the moonstruck images. I had seen them for quite some time, normally in deep meditation, where, with few exceptions, the moonstruck people or scenes are played out at an incredible speed. They are shadows or geometric blotches upon a colored canvas of the mind. They serve as a download of information, a symbolic code that holds the keys to unlocking parts of the mind. The blotches are so precise that if consciously seen, one intuitively knows that they cannot possibly be random.

It is difficult to go into detail because of the rate at which the images are passing before the mind and the incredible level of detail contained in the images. They are beyond description. The scenes remind me of how people describe near death experiences, where their lives flash before their eyes, except my moonstruck images are not scenes from this lifetime. Many are simply intricate geometric patterns holding incredible amounts of detail.

On this morning, I was serenaded by two identical moonstruck twins wearing short mini-skirts that reminded me of the little skirts that cheerleaders wear. Unlike other times, these images were different. The scenes were being played out at normal speed and were accompanied by music. The twins were facing each other doing some song and dance routine. The twin on the left squatted down and when he stood up his skirt unraveled and came down like the loose fitting pants worn by karate fighters.

I then opened my eyes and thought, "Boy, that was weird." I wondered where these images came from. I then started to pay attention to the words of their song, "Wrapped around your finger." Then I heard the other twin sing the chorus, "Wrapped around your finger-er-er." Another difference with today's moonstruck images was that aside from being played out at normal speed the twins possessed rough facial features. They were coming to life. They were now more than simply shadow images.

I closed my eyes again and meditated a bit more to see what other messages they might have for me. I continued to watch them. Even though they were not in full living color they did have an incredible amount of detail. They were standing on a beach against moonstruck palm trees. The backdrop colors were a blend of red and orange with hints of yellow, and of course, black as the opposite color. No other colors were present. I then noticed that the one on the left was holding a microphone in one hand as he danced to this duet. It was so cute; they reminded me of Milli Vanilli. I opened my eyes again in utter amazement. I then thought, "What are you doing? Close your eyes and get as much information as possible." I closed my eyes and continued to see my Milli Vanilli players enjoying their little song and dance.

As if that was not enough, I suddenly saw a man of about the age of 32 appear before me. It felt as if I was in a movie theatre and someone, "the man," had walked up to take a seat in front of me. I could see him from the waist up. The man was a beautiful ageless translucent blue spirit. He bore an incredible resemblance to me. He could easily be my twin, with the exception that this guy was 10 times as good looking. He was remarkably ageless in his beauty. If I had a prime of my life...he was it. I could see right through him to the backdrop of my Milli Vanilli video playing in the background. His eyes held an incredible amount of love and light. He gently gazed at me and smiled. This was our song and dance, our movie being played out upon the stage of life. He, my twin, was wrapped around my finger and I around his. He was my Higher Self.

THE HIGHER SELF

Kiss To Build a Dream on – Timothy and the Indian Chief

I had a dream this morning where my mother is sleeping in my bed. I keep telling her that she cannot sleep in my bed. "You can't sleep here, you can't sleep here." She insists upon sleeping in my bed. I feel pressured to share my bed, which I do not want to do. I then feel someone from behind me say, "Just get in bed and lay on your back." "Lay on your back," I hear a man say again forcefully.

The struggle woke me up. When I opened my eyes there was an Indian Chief standing next to my bed. He was looking at the ceiling praying. He had both hands together next to his mouth like the images everyone has seen of Christ's hands in prayer. He had a large headdress of feathers that reached over his head and were draped down his back. I assumed he was the one insisting I lay on my back. I did not know what to think, but since he was praying I assumed he was not looking to hurt me.

I took his suggestion and laid on my back and began to meditate. The only time I lie on my back in bed is when I meditate, so I took the suggestion as meaning that I should meditate. Normally, I hate lying on my back.

I closed my eyes and relaxed. As my meditative state deepened, I saw a vision of my Indian Chief performing what looked to be ritual dance. I could see his headdress going up and down. The image was in moonstruck form. I then felt as if I were in someone's company. While in meditation, I could see surrounding me two other people watching the Indian dance with me. It was almost as if they were sitting on the edge of my bed. They each turned and smiled at me. I noticed they each wore a numbered jersey. The one to my left had the number 12 and the other directly in front of me had the number 19. I began hearing that old Louis Armstrong song, "Kiss to Build a Dream On." Then I heard someone call out the name Timothy.

IN THE COURSE OF A DREAM EMANUEL FOR LOVE

Not wanting to miss any of this, I grabbed my voice recorder to record the details for later research. I immediately caught on to the numerology associated with the numbers on the jerseys, 12 being equal to 3 and 19 being equal to 1. Could it be that the guy who wore the number 1 jersey was God and the guy who wore the number 3 jersey was Christ?

When I woke up I looked for the Louis Armstrong song and I purchased it online. It is not a song I would have bought before today. I took my iPod with me to listen to the song on my way to church. What a beautiful song. I later found out the song was in the soundtrack to the movie, "Sleepless in Seattle." How ironic. I just know one day someone will make a movie out of my book. This is incredible stuff. This is a New York Times best seller ready to make into a Hollywood movie.

I know this work was made to touch the lives of many. I cannot contain the joy within me. If nothing else, it will be online for all to read someday after I am dead and gone. Someone someday will say, "Yeah, what was his name....the Dreamer guy? What was his name?" Then I will simply be remembered as, "The Dreamer."

I played the song over and over again. Was someone in heaven sending me a kiss on which to build my dream on? "Sealed with a Kiss," how romantic. I feel like I am falling in love with someone I do not even know. What I do know is that he is quite playful. I am so enamored by him. I love God with every fabric of my being!

I arrived early again for church to take advantage of the free Reiki before service. During my Reiki I had the most incredible vision. I felt I was in heaven. I saw someone seated with his head bent over, like when they tell you on a plane to put your arms around the life vest and assume the crash position. I wanted to know why he was in this position. Was he in pain or was he asleep?

The Higher Self

Slowly he lifted his head and leaned back in his chair. From the center of his chest a hole opened up. I approached closer for a better look. The hole in his chest was now a black hole through which I could see the outermost recesses of our galaxy.

Blue rays of light began to show forth from a solitary star deep within this man's chest. The light then took on the form of a tiny little man who began walking toward me. As he approached, the blue and white rays of light intensified like a welder's torch. I then knew it was Christ. All I could focus on was the intensity of the light. He came closer and closer and I could not back away, until finally his presence engulfed me and I could see him no more. We were one and I was at peace.

I was not sure what the name Timothy meant. I thought it might be from the Bible but I could not be sure. I looked it up and there are two letters in the Bible that Paul wrote to Timothy. I read both and they addressed all the reservations I had in my heart. It was almost as if Paul was speaking directly to me. It had meaning for me personally; an answer to a prayer. Over and over the message is clear in my heart. Christ has come. He calls upon me to awaken from the dream. "AWAKEN, MY LOVED ONE, AWAKEN."

As I reflect back on this dream I have to wonder if maybe my Indian Chief was not an Indian at all. Could he have been an angel sent from God? Could that feathered headdress that rose so predominately over his head have actually been the feathers of his wings?

Timothy answers my "Why me?" question but it still remains inconceivable that he chose me to carry this message. The rapture I feel could only be God's presence in my life. If I could only find a way to share this, there would be instant peace in the world, for everyone would know they are loved unconditionally exactly as they are. I know I am *SO LOVED*. Just look at me and where I have come from. We are all equal and there is a place for everyone in Heaven, even people like me.

Who's That Man in the Window?

On this day, I was visiting friends and family up in Albany. It was morning and I could hear everyone talking in the kitchen. I tried to get up but kept falling back to sleep. I finally thought to myself, "Enough sleep, I need to get up." I tried to keep myself from falling asleep again but I could not. I then had a false awakening. I could see that I was in the spare bedroom where I was visiting. The window above my head was open. In my dream I looked up at the ceiling and heard Joe and his mom out in the front yard on the deck. I then heard someone fussing with the window. I thought Joe was trying to pull a prank on me so I was prepared. I looked up again and saw the mini blinds lift and a young man with black hair and a small mustache standing outside looking at me through the window. I thought I had better tell Mama that someone was snooping in her windows. I tried to move but could not. I kept struggling but my body just would not move. Finally, I woke up and realized that the man in the window was a dream. I had just had a false awakening.

As I reflected back on the dream I recognized the man as me at around the age of 23. Windows in dreams have always provided an opportunity for me to have a glimpse into other dimensions of myself. I know that the man had to have been my Higher Self making his presence known to me. He always keeps a watchful eye on me.

The Twin Sisters Share the Same Make-Up Artist

Last night I had a dream where I am at a fashion show that my friend Toni is in. She is all dressed up and looking beautiful. The event is extremely colorful. There are twin sisters appearing in the show, who are the most beautiful of all the models. There are subtle differences in their appearances but for all intensive purposes they are identical twins. They have golden blond hair and deep cocoa butter tans. They are absolutely radiant with rosy flesh tones that come through their cocoa butter skin as if they have just come in from the sun. They model different outfits on the runway. Everyone came here today to specifically see these two models.

One of the girls has on an outfit that includes a golden serpentine veil that she wears over her face. I am surprised that she is able to see through the veil to walk the runway with ease and grace. Since my friend Toni is also a model in the show, I am allowed to visit backstage while the models are getting ready. In between wardrobe changes and without makeup, I notice the twin girls look quite average. Somehow the fashion show designers and coordinators were able to see their hidden beauty and full potential. The twin sisters also share the same makeup artist. She is a vibrant and beautiful young woman. Interestingly, her face is blue and her hair is jet black. She looks absolutely stunning. I catch her profile as she turns to look toward me. As I watch her, she gently pushes her hair back with her fingers from about her right eye. I am struck by how perfect her eyebrows were done. Her eye makeup is simply exquisite. Her craft is so perfected that she is able to cause these two average looking girls to be transformed into stunning runway models for the fashion industry. These twins are the most sought after models for their exquisite beauty and grace on the runway. I also notice the girls are very humble about the inner beauty that they naturally carry.

I see Joe at the event but he is not the adult I know him to be in real life. Here he is a young child. Knowing he must be looking for me, I walk up to him and look down upon his innocent face. I tell him that I am very sorry that it did not work out between us. I must move on and go forward with my life and my spiritual pursuits. I turn and walk away, leaving Joe behind and never looking back.

I then head home to a family reunion. I arrive at my family's house in California. I decide to surprise everyone by coming in through the side entrance. As I walk up, I can see all the buffet tables and my father standing in the distance. I am happy to be home. Before I even reach the gate, they see me coming up the walk and everyone starts shouting, "He's here, he's here, he has arrived."

We are our own messiah. It does not matter through which door we enter into our father's house, he awaits within. I love the way this dream speaks about the twin flame and the serpentine veil. My twin flame is none other than my Higher Self. We share a third eye, the gift of the Holy Spirit who colors our world and allows us to discover our inner beauty. The journey sometimes requires us to leave behind childish ways to pursue knowledge of the spirit.

You Are a Real Steve McQueen

I had a dream in which many years had passed. I am going back to visit my first partner, Jerry, who is now living with my old roommate, Larry, on Mount Washington. When I arrive, I see that Jerry is now in a relationship with someone who is trying to live his life as if he were me. He thinks that for Jerry to like him, he has to fill my shoes. I guess Jerry, missing his one true love, namely me, has settled on someone who reminds him of me. In essence, Jerry wants what we once had. However, the guy he found is a shady character at best, in his dealings. He plays as a good person when in actuality he is doing things that are against the law. I can tell that Jerry is not quite happy in his relationship because he walks around dazed and in a fog.

THE HIGHER SELF

I look around the house where I once lived. It is such a nice place high on a hill. The living space is very comfortable and more than anyone could really ask for. As we sit, we suddenly hear helicopters circling overhead. Searchlights are now upon the house, shining in through the skylights above. I hear a voice on the loudspeaker say, "You are under arrest." I look around thinking they cannot be talking to us. However, they storm the house and handcuff Jerry's boyfriend to haul him away. Jerry is left with no one to love.

I think, "Now that this guy is gone and can never pose a threat to anyone or me, maybe I should reconsider and come back to live on the mountain. It is a beautiful place and there is everything I could ever want here, with free room and board, if I can live with the one exception that this home would not be my own, for it belongs to Larry."

The only thing I do not know is how Jerry feels about living in Larry's home, since Jerry always wanted a house of his own. Jerry tells me that Larry is never home. Larry allows him free reign to do anything he pleases with the house. It is as if it were his.

"Besides," he says, "Larry was really good looking at one time." Jerry then shows me a movie in which Larry starred at the prime of his life. I did not know Larry had been a movie star and a good one at that. He has a great deal of hidden talent. I watch the video and I cannot believe that Larry, my old roommate, is a former movie star. I never knew he had a career in the motion picture industry. Wow, I can now see that it is true, Larry was one hot stud in his day, a real Steve McQueen.

As luck would have it, in walks my old roommate, Larry. I holler, "Hey Larry, long time no see."

I am very happy to see him. In looking at him, I realize Larry has not changed a bit in all these years. He is still incredibly hot with a hint of distinguished graying around the temples. I think I just might consider coming back to live on Mount Washington.

Our true relationship is with God and our Higher Self, our First Love. Caught up in the illusion, we allow the ego to fill our shoes, dictate our lives and cast shadows, which we then fear. Believing in shadows, we look to them for the love we once had.

Turning our attention to the Light of Heaven, we realize we are gods. In God's image we were cast, inseparable from the whole. Not until we are shown the videotapes are we reminded of all the many movies in which we played the starring role. In the fullness of our beauty we stand to inherit the kingdom within.

Who Are You? The Wormhole Dragon

This morning I woke up at 8 am. I decided to go ahead and let the dogs out. When we were all done relieving ourselves, we crawled back in bed for another hour of precious sleep. I had no sooner laid my head on my pillow when I had a false awakening. In front of me I could see my closet door. I noticed something unusual. The closet door had a mail slot. I instantly knew this was in fact a false awakening.

Curious to know what might be on the other side of the mail slot, I decided to move in closer to attempt to peak through it. I pushed my finger through the mail slot, lifting the door just enough to see the other side. On the other side everything was pitch black; total and complete darkness. Puzzled, I tried to figure out this new mystery before me. A part of me was not satisfied with what I saw. I decided to try looking once again to see if anything had changed. Again I pushed the mail slot open with my finger. I could still see there was blackness but this time I saw that the darkness was caused by a black curtain or veil that had been draped over the mail slot to prevent me from seeing the other side.

The Higher Self

Not knowing what to do with this puzzle, I laid back within my physical body to think. I then remembered that I had been successful at having out of body experiences associated with false awakenings before. I decided I would try to pull myself completely away from my body. I tried to move but kept hitting a wall as if I were encased in a glass aquarium. I relaxed and took a couple of deep breaths. Miraculously, I began to float away and out of my body. I soon left the room and began to travel in what appeared to be deep space. I could see a network of wormholes.

I traveled through these wormholes at an incredible speed. Every once in a while, I would see a fork, where I could choose which direction I wanted to go. I finally came out of the wormhole and found myself on a planet with prehistoric creatures, dinosaurs of some kind. My consciousness came to rest upon the surface of the planet. I was in the middle of chaos. My entry into their world had startled the reptilians and now they were all running mad. One of the dinosaurs flung its tail at me. I could see the tail coming toward me at an incredible speed. I was not afraid. I braced for impact. Upon impact I felt the tail of the creature go through me but I was unharmed.

Wanting to get out of there, I took flight and headed for the wormholes again. There were beings guarding the entrance into the network of wormholes. I was determined to enter and refused to be held back. I tried to bulldoze my way through. I flew at an incredible speed toward those guarding the entrance. They all saw me coming and were in shock. As I flew passed them, I caught a glimpse of my shadow. My shadow was that of a great big bird with an incredible wingspan. I understood now why they feared me.

I entered the wormhole. As I flew, I lifted my head to see straight ahead. It was the most incredible experience I have ever seen. There was so much light coming through the wormhole. Great blue stars were everywhere whisking past me. I was in total awe. When I came out there was a fire breathing mythical dragon flying below me. I could see the red flames coming out of his mouth. I wanted to enter in through the mouth of the dragon because I believed it would have given way to another wormhole but instead I decided to mount the dragon.

As I mounted the dragon, we descended at great speed as though I was simply too much weight for the dragon to carry. We plummeted into the underworld where it was apparent the people here were enslaved. People walked around aimless, dazed, asleep and with no real hope. Yet these people did not realize their slavery because it was what they had been born into. They lived in darkness, unable to see.

I felt a compelling urge to help them realize their entrapment. I hovered over these people but they could not see me. I looked deep into their faces and still they could not see me. Not even their captors could see me. Then I saw one man who came stumbling toward me. He appeared to be sleepwalking. His eyes were rolled back in his head, yet he could somehow see me. I backed away to see if he would follow. I moved to the left and then the right. Without a doubt, he could see me. No matter where I moved, he followed. His captors around him did not suspect anything because they knew he was sleepwalking. I finally allowed him to catch up to me. He grabbed my arms and held on tight. As he held me, I could feel his grip.

I looked into his face and asked, "Who are you?"

His face became illuminated with a pastel shade of gray and everyone around him began to notice that he had found something. Knowing I could not bring him with me, I simply opened my eyes.

I laid in bed in total disbelief of all I had just experienced. I immediately wanted to go back to do something for those people. I just did not

The Higher Self

know what I could possibly do. The captors had sealed off the wormholes by camouflaging the openings so that no one would escape. If the people did not know the wormholes existed they would never think to look for them. If I could somehow expose the wormholes I might be able to communicate a message back to them.

I closed my eyes again and found myself hovering over the place I had been previously. I then heard a voice. The voice sounded like one I have heard guiding me many times, but this time the message it had was not a loving one. I knew this had to be the voice of the dark side. The captors had become aware of my presence and knew I would come back.

I could see how they had selfishly taken all access to the wormholes for themselves. Their ships could come and go as they pleased. Yet those enslaved were denied access. I moved around and studied their operations. I wanted to go through the wormholes their ships were using to find out where they lead to. I could see right through the camouflage they used. I decided to try it and go through their wormholes. As I tried to enter, I hit my head on a glass enclosure. They had sealed the wormholes with glass. I knew from hitting my head on glass before that it would only hold me back temporarily. If I truly believed, I could will myself to go through. I then heard the voice again say, "Come on, you know you're going to do it."

This dream/vision was told through the eyes of my Higher Self who holds the promise of the Holy Spirit. I now see my Higher Self and the Holy Spirit to be one and the same, as I am in my Father and my Father is in me. The Holy Spirit is One with my Higher Self. Everything around me is returning to a state of oneness.

IN THE COURSE OF A DREAM EMANUEL FOR LOVE

When I, through the eyes of my Higher Self, descended into the underworld I saw my physical existence for what it really is. I realized the man who grabbed the arm of my Higher Self was me. I remembered back to that morning. I was the one who was struggling to see, desperately fighting to follow in the Light and footsteps of my Higher Self wherever he may lead.

Our ticket out of slavery is to regain the means by which to travel inter-dimensionally through the network of wormholes. That awareness of the wormholes and the means to use them comes from working the dream space and learning how to live life fully lucid. We can be fully alive on every dimension in which we exist. Those dimensions are as real as our physical reality and are not solely confined to our dreams. They can be experienced by our waking consciousness. Our ticket to freedom comes from harnessing the dream space. It simply must be done in order to come into the fullness of being.

We have become enslaved by our own fears and the illusions they create. We are held hostage by all who subscribe to the dark side and who, through greed and the pursuit of power, unknowingly rob us of our birthright to travel and experience the universe. This condition need not persist. These wormholes hold our rite of passage into other dimensions of existence. We must awaken to rise up to multi-dimensional awareness and discover the fullness of who we really are. We are ready. The time has come. Hear the call; Awaken!

You are the Most Beautiful Woman I Have Ever Seen

I was in great pain today. One of my two toy poodles, my chocolate male named Babers, passed away last night. He had been vomiting for a couple of days. I finally took him to the vet to have him checked. They kept him overnight to run some tests on him. They determined he was suffering from pancreatic inflammation. We tried a blood transfusion but in the end he did not respond positively to the procedure. His condition deteriorated and I was forced to make the painful decision to end his precious little life. He died in my arms. My heart was crushed. I cried and asked him to please forgive me. He was 12 years old. He had been with me nearly his entire life. Never a day went by that I did not wake with his breath in my ear.

After coming home from the animal hospital I placed a small framed picture of Babers on my nightstand with an amethyst crystal, my birthstone, beside it. I prayed that I would see him in my dreams. The night went by and when I awoke in the morning I had not had a dream about him. I got out of bed to let my other apricot toy poodle, Butters, out to do his business. When he was done we retired to the bedroom for a quiet mediation. I had no sooner laid my head on the pillow and closed my eyes when I had a false awakening.

I found myself sitting in the library when I heard a knock on the door. I could see my neighbor Evelyn peeking through the side window to see if anyone was home. It was the day she normally comes to clean my house. I got up to open the door and proceeded to tell her about Babers. As I was telling her the news, I noticed she was much shorter than usual and her complexion was a dark chocolate brown. This was not the Evelyn I knew in real life so I assumed I was having a false awakening. I knew this was my chance to go look for Babers.

I walked out my front door and a young boy between 12 and 15 years of age came rushing over toward me. He looked at me with love in his eyes and said, "You are the most beautiful woman I have ever seen." Bewildered, I took a step back and in so doing noticed my hooded robe that caressed my face. I was wearing a bright yellow robe much like the one I had seen my guardian angel wear.

In that moment I thought to myself, "Why would he think I'm a woman?" Then I realized, "I'm apparently an angel." Remembering the times when I had seen angels, I knew they often reflected what is inside me that I have projected onto them. Knowing the robes they wear are like mirrors unto the soul, I allowed this little boy to see me as it was in his heart to project.

Realizing I was called to be his angel in spirit, I reached out and placed my hand on his upper arm. To my surprise he was not formless. I felt his physical presence within the grip of my hand. I could see my outstretched arm, which was milky white in color, draped with a glowing yellow robe. He then said to me, "I would love to have a pair of earrings much like yours."

The earrings I wear are not easily removed so instead of giving him mine, I reached out and held his earlobes between my thumb and forefinger. As I removed my hand, transparent earrings appeared on him. Satisfied, he turned and rushed off into the dark of night. As I watched, I noticed a silver cord trailing him. Rainbow colors pulsated within the silver cord. I followed the silver cord back in my direction and realized our beings were tethered to each other by this silver cord. From the still of night, I heard him call back to me, "I forgive you." I instantly knew this boy was my little man, my precious little Babers.

I then ran forward, following the silver cord, to see him one last time. As I ran, my robe caught sail and my body took flight. In amazement, I looked around and to the right and left of me I saw massive outstretched silver wings the size of aircraft. How could these be my wings? I could feel the wind rushing about my body. I heard a voice that said, "Look to your far right." I turned to look and in the distance I saw a little angel in flight next to me

THE HIGHER SELF

watching over me. Between us was the silver cord that tethered us to one another.

Knowing it was Babers, I dropped into a state of utter bliss. I saw the shores of a beautiful ocean and a scenic coastline on a pristine day, in full and vivid detail. We soared high in the sky, then began to descend toward the ocean below. We swam among the fish of the sea.

I watched him swimming in the distance. He swam further and further into a dark abyss. Not wanting to go into the darkness of the abyss with him, I decided to pull on the silver cord and reel him in toward me. As I reeled him in, I heard a voice say, "He knows not what he does." I then saw a dragon surface from the abyss. Refusing to lose him within the darkness of the abyss, I placed my hand upon the forehead of the dragon and visualized the image of Christ in my mind. Light then came to the depths of the abyss. The dragon turned to clay and shattered into a million pieces and sank to the bottom of the abyss. In the light, I then saw my little angel sitting peacefully in the distance.

The next day while in meditation, I still yearned to see my little man. I began having a vision in which I saw a meadow and there was rustling within the many plants of the field. Suddenly I saw the shadow of a little dog much like Babers. I followed the shadow until I came upon the little dog in a clearing. He marched happily among the tall grasses. I then saw that upon the ends of the earth stood a man completely naked and larger than life, whose image was impressed upon the heavens. He called to the dog, who quickly ran to his side content to follow him. I recognized this man to be my Higher Self.

I am blessed to have loved such a precious gift as my little man Babers. Much like my Higher Self, he won my heart without ever uttering a word. He has taught me what it is to love unconditionally. He has taught me how to walk in his master's shadow and serve with a faithful heart. He has reminded me that I too am someone's little man.

It's a Miracle; High on Life

Joseph the Master of Dreams

Last night before going to bed I decided to watch one of my History Channel videotapes, Mysteries of the Bible. I bought the complete two-box set of about 12 VHS tapes many years ago, which I still have today. I had not watched them in a long time so I decided to watch one of the tapes titled, "*Joseph.*" Not having read the smaller print, I assumed it referred to Joseph and Mary. As I went to insert the tape in the VCR, my eye caught a glance at the subheading, "*Master of Dreams.*" Instantly this title sparked an immense curiosity. I thought, "Who was this 'Joseph, Master of Dreams?'" When I put the tape in and the introduction began, it became clear that I had my Josephs crossed. This was not about Mary's Joseph, but about Joseph the son of Jacob from the book of Genesis, who was sold by his brothers into slavery. My recollection of the story all came pouring back.

Watching the documentary this time around, I found the story to have a striking resemblance to my life. I identified with the story. Joseph was Jacob's favorite son because he had him in his old age. I, like Joseph, am my mother's favorite son for the same reason. My mother was 38 years old when she gave birth to me. Joseph's father Jacob gave him a very special coat to wear of rainbow colors. I saw the coat to be symbolic of the rainbow colored night lights that I see in my meditations and visions when I lie snuggly under my bed comforter. A coat or comforter is also said to be the symbol of the Holy Spirit. I know it is the Holy Spirit within my night lights that guides me on this journey of self-actualization and enlightenment through experiencing my dreams. Could it be that when I nestle under my bed sheets at night to dream that I am actually nestling within the Holy Spirit? There is a Universal Truth in the Bible that says God will send the comforter, the Holy Spirit, to guide us and we will come to know it inwardly by the still small voice.

Joseph had a dream that he translated to mean that his brothers would one day bow before him. He had a second dream that he translated to mean that his parents too would one day bow before him. I believe these prophetic dreams not only came to pass in the time of Joseph but are also coming to pass as this new Age of Aquarius dawns. If Joseph is placed as the symbol for the dream then the day is here when we must now come to bow before our dreams, our inner altar within the heart and mind, as we learn the true purpose for which dreams were given us. This is the same dream we sold into slavery and have long forgotten. Universal Truths are those Truths viewed symbolically whose relationships are multi-dimensional. No matter how you view this Truth, the Ambigram always holds true. We are God's Truth; we are the Ambigram; we are the living image of God. Our dreams speak this language with which we may come to know our multi-dimensional nature, the role we play in the greater whole and our Higher Self. I am now, in the face of my own Truth, able to view my own Ambigram. It is God becoming aware of its Self within me, its Higher Self, a Self we all have. It is the most beautiful and wonderful thing one could ever imagine or experience. It produces a NATURAL HIGH that is beyond words. It places one in a state of complete and utter bliss.

These dreams angered Joseph's brothers and one day his brothers set out to kill Joseph. Fortunately, Rueben, the first born son of Jacob whose name I share, intervened on Joseph's behalf and spared the life of his younger brother. Ironically, I too see myself as Rueben interceding on behalf of Joseph, beckoning humanity to pay attention to their dreams. While Rueben is away, the other brothers sell their brother Joseph to slave traders. We live with many different brothers inside of us, all of whom have their own agenda. These are dimensions of awareness in which we exist. We are all guilty of having sold our dreams to slavery. Filling the spiritual void is to reconcile our splintered self and restore our being to its full multi-dimensional nature. It is the missing piece to realizing and actualizing our own divinity. The spiritual void we experience is caused by that fact that we have not fully resolved the Joseph issue. We place little to no importance on our dreams thereby ignoring Joseph altogether. In the story when Rueben returns, Joseph is gone. When we return from a good night's sleep, isn't Joseph gone?

Very few people place any conscious effort on recalling their dreams. Parents do not encourage their children to do so either. This vital link to our Divine essence withers. We cannot return home without bringing Joseph back with us. This is my purpose -- to proclaim that Joseph is alive and to bring him home that you may see and know him.

Joseph is sent to Egypt by the slave traders, where he is wrongly accused and thrown in prison. In some way, I feel I too have lived for many years enslaved by my own addictions and fears. While in prison, Joseph has the opportunity to interpret one of the dreams of one of the inmates. The interpretation proves to be accurate and the inmate is released from prison and promises to remember Joseph. Several years pass till one day the Pharaoh has a troubling dream and no one is able to interpret the dream. The inmate then remembers Joseph and tells the Pharaoh who then summons Joseph to come and interpret his dream. The dream is interpreted by Joseph to mean that Egypt will receive seven years of good harvest followed by seven years of famine. The Pharaoh then appoints Joseph as his advisor and places him in charge of distributing the grains of wheat to feed the people.

This last part is chocked full of symbolism that rings true for me in a very personal way. I too am responsible for distributing the wheat but in my case it is the message of the wheat penny contained in this book. It is the magic of synchronicity when enlightened by the dream. When we pay attention to our dreams the number of synchronicities, magical moments and "ah ha" experiences increase. To truly be fed by the Holy Spirit and to see the wheat penny effect in our lives, we need to cultivate our dreams for messages from Spirit. Spirit will not leave us hungry if we earnestly seek with an open mind and an open heart. Our future is bright. We will come of age, for in the end Joseph's family was reunited and he achieved worldly recognition and power through his association with the Pharaoh.

The Whirling Dervish's Big Idea

I laid down to sleep and began my normal meditation process but this time I decided to try to meditate with my eyes open. I meditated for what seemed to be a very long time. Interestingly, I must have drifted off into some kind of trance because toward the end of the meditation I had the sense of waking up. I was puzzled. How I could be waking up if I had not yet closed my eyes? I wondered if it was possible to fall asleep with my eyes open and become lucid. I did not want to disturb what was happening so I remained calm and relaxed and simply observed my surroundings, consciously preserving my mental state. I was clearly in my bedroom. I sensed something going on in the distance. I could see what appeared to be a remote viewing screen that had a movie playing on it. The mental screen began to drift slowly in my direction and I could clearly see what looked like three whirling dervishes. Each whirling dervish was partnered with a cartoon hippopotamus that it spun in the air above its head. One of the dervishes was fiercely twirling his hippo so fast that the hippo flew loose from his hand and into the air and was catapulted out of the remote viewing screen and into the open space of my bedroom. I heard a popping sound as the hippo came flying out of the remote viewing screen and into the air toward me. The little hippo stopped short of hitting the wall above my headboard. He continued his little dance floating above my head. I named him Potamus. In the distance, I could see the dervishes dancing happily on the still floating screen.

Now I too had my own little hippo above my head. It was so delightful to watch Potamus dance as he kicked his heels up in the air while filled with joy and happiness. I stared at little Potamus who was clearly very excited to be dancing above my head. He was dancing and jumping head over heels. Then around the room, I began to see several bright blue orbs enter from the ceiling and descend into my room. Each orb shined forth a magnificent blue halo. Then I saw green angel hair begin to fill the room. I looked beside my bed at what appeared to be an angelic presence. I could not tell if it was a man or a woman but I could definitely see a figure of a person beside my bed. From the mouth of the apparition blew forth a bright red fireball. It was clearly very happy to have entertained me. I closed my eyes, praised the Lord and fell gently to sleep.

Later when I awoke I wanted to know the meaning of the Dervish so I looked it up on Wikipedia. I found the following:

> *"The Mevlevi, or 'The Whirling Dervishes,' believe in performing their dhikr in the form of a 'dance' and music ceremony called the Sema. The Sema represents a mystical journey of man's spiritual ascent through mind and love to 'Perfect.' Turning towards the truth, the follower grows through love, deserts his ego, finds the truth and arrives to the 'Perfect.' He then returns from this spiritual journey as a*

man who has reached maturity and a greater perfection, so as to love and to be of service to the whole of creation."

Before ever coming into this physical existence I had an idea for this lifetime, a gift I wished to bring to humanity. Through my power to create, I placed it in the form I called Potamus. He remained just below the surface of the water where he was safe until the time was right for me to execute that part of my Divine purpose. Potamus has helped me wake up and reacquaint myself with the Divine Plan and my original intent for my life. It is in coming to that awareness that Christ is again born in the heart and mind because Potamus was born of Love. Potamus also serves to remind me that it need not all be so serious. The process was meant to be fun and uplifting. We can lighten up our hearts and relieve ourselves of the burdens, the weight we carry, by submerging ourselves in the eternal bliss that comes from the awareness of our Divine purpose.

Potamus Teaches Me the Art of Feng Shui and the Power of Suggestion

Last night while in meditation, I slipped into a false awakening where I could clearly see my bedroom. I noticed one of my closet doors was cracked open. There was a spirit hiding behind my closet doors. I knew this because I could see the spirit's incredibly pudgy toes sticking out from under the door. I stood there for a second not knowing what to do. "Should I open the door and face the spirit or simply make as if I am unaware of its presence?"

I hesitated for a moment, doubting I had sufficient courage to confront whatever was in there. I decided to investigate. For a measure of safety, I stood a few steps away from the door just far enough to be able to reach the door knob. I took a deep breath and grabbed the door knob and quickly pulled the door open. The door swung open to reveal what seemed to be a pitch black interior.

My fear kept me one step away from being able to get a good look inside. I knew the spirit was in there tucked away in a corner of the closet because I could still see its toes. I thought to myself, "Okay, you can do this, Ruben. Get closer and take a good look at this spirit's face. Do it! Do it now!" If I was going to poop my pants with fear, I figured the least I could do is bring back a positive identification to nab this mischievous spirit. I came in closer and zeroed in on the chap's eyes peaking through the darkness.

As I got closer my heart began to melt. The fellow looked scared. His face was old and wrinkled. I could see his eyes, cheeks and complexion as he turned to look away and hide. He looked very grey and tired. I thought, "Could this be what dead people look like?" This guy was an odd looking fellow who apparently had a few extra pounds on him. I then caught a glimpse of his lips. I had a sudden sense that he wanted to lick me like my dogs do when I wake up in the morning.

I pulled back in spirit and screamed, "OOOH NO! You're ugly." We both ran in opposite directions. I then turned around to see where he had gone and could see him running fast in the distance. It was Potamus! I yelled out to him, "Please don't go, Potamus, I'm sorry I thought you were ugly. You scared me. Please forgive me."

The difference this time was that he had shed some of his cartoon-ish qualities and had taken on more life-like attributes. He was now becoming a real hippo. I could see him running back toward the swamp for cover. In my mind I yelled out, "Wait, wait, I'm sorry. I didn't know it was you. Come back!!" I could see a door open in the forest. He ran for the door and it slammed shut behind him. I thought, "OH NO, I have unknowingly offended my friend Potamus."

I saw a little of myself in him and remembered back to when I was growing up. My aunts would jokingly make mean comments to me telling me I was ugly. I remember how much that hurt. I did not want to hurt anyone. I realized that Potamus was a reflection of me.

I then saw the door in the forest open again and out came my cartoon Potamus dancing and twirling. He was celebrating that I had just been taught a lesson. Potamus had been teaching me a lesson on fear and the power of suggestion.

Words carry with them unseen power. A simple suggestion has the power to change the course of events. We need to be mindful of what we say and not leave negative suggestions hanging in our closets for us to later wear around as if they are a part of us. We need not fear those parts of ourselves that we have been overly critical of. We can approach ourselves with loving eyes and return to a state of child-like innocence where playing in the closet was fun. When we need a miracle in our lives we need only hold on to positive thoughts, intentions and affirmations.

During the night I woke up several times to go to the restroom. On one of those occasions, I laid back down and resumed my meditation. I then began to see moonstruck images on an orange canvas within my mind. The dark blotches were definite patterns. One pattern looked like a lizard. It kept recurring and appearing in different positions on the canvas of my mind. The images were appearing, disappearing and reappearing in rapid succession. My mind was learning how to decipher the placement of patterns for meaning. What I was seeing was a language or type of Morse code like Egyptian hieroglyphics, where it was not just the symbol that had meaning but also the placement of that symbol on the canvas of my mind -- a Feng Shui of symbols. The orange was so bright with perfect black blotches.

The patterns then stopped and all I could see was a bright white light. This light was so bright I felt like my eyes were open and staring directly at the noon-day sun except I knew my eyes were closed and it was the middle of the night. This light was the Light of Christ within me. I knew this because it came with an incredible sense of inner peace. I opened my eyes and looked around the room. There was no light anywhere in my room. I once again closed my eyes and immediately returned to the Light of Christ before my eyes. The Light enveloped my entire being and I fell into an eternal state of utter bliss.

The subconscious mind is where the code is stored to activate our DNA and transform us into beings of Light. We need look no further than within the Self. There is only one key that will unlock our true potential. The key is not shared among many. It is unique to each one of us. Use of the key lifts the veil of separation and brings us back into the awareness of our original state of oneness. It brings us back to our God Self.

The Family Portrait

I laid in bed and began my meditation. I then had a vision where I saw the faces of a family who were in the middle of a portrait sitting. I was captivated by the mother who sat in the center. She was approximately 30 years old and stunningly beautiful with wavy shoulder length black hair and an olive complexion. I was quite enamored by this woman's beauty. She was simple but radiated the most incredible beauty and a profound sense of love and kindness. I was beside myself at the level of detail with which my mind was forming the images of people I had never seen before. I wondered where these images came from.

In the morning on the drive to the office, I was thinking about the vision and it hit me. Something inside told me this woman was "my mother." I daydreamed about how wonderful it would be to have the opportunity to have my mother in my presence for one day at her youthful age of 30. I thought of the many things I would teach her and the chance at giving her a better life. To simply enjoy her company was a thought very pleasing to me. I felt so fortunate to have been able to see her image as she was then. I remembered the way she moved and her gaze as she looked at me.

When I got to work, I quickly forgot about the dream in the busy-ness of my day. Around noon my computer locked up and I had to reboot. While I waited for it to reboot, I decided to take the opportunity and call my mother. She answered the phone and said, "What a coincidence." She had just been thinking about me. She proceeded to tell me that she had had an incredible dream. I had already completely forgotten that I too had seen "my mother" in my meditation that morning.

Excited about her dream, I asked her to tell me about it. She told me that she found herself walking along the beach with me on a beautiful day where the sun was high and bright in the sky. She said she had held my hand as we walked along the beach and talked. She remarked how vivid and beautiful the dream was. She said it felt so good to be in my presence. My memory clicked and I shared with her the vision I had while in meditation of the woman whom I later recognized as "my mother" and how stunningly beautiful she was. She reminded me that it could not have been her because she did not give birth to me until she was 38. She said it must have been a vision of the Virgin Mary.

It's a Miracle; High on Life

I told her, "No, Mom, it was you." She then proceeded to tell me the rest of her dream. She dreamt that she had asked my brother Paz to let her have his cell phone, which he never uses, to call us and her sisters (my aunts) whenever she wants to. I then told her about my having seen the spirit of my grandmother in my house not long ago. I told Mom what I have come to know about the power of dreams and why I believed she had this dream. This dream served to remind us that no matter where we are we remain in constant communication with each other and the rest of our heavenly family. I told her to promise me that when she passes on she will visit me in my dreams. I told her to practice now remembering her dreams.

Madonna Wants to Meet the Dreamer

I had a dream the night before the vision of The Family Portrait. I had recorded the details of the earlier dream on my voice recorder but had forgotten all about it. I did not get around to journaling it until after I had journaled the vision of the portrait sitting. Interestingly enough, this earlier dream relates directly to the vision in a very mystical and magical way.

This dream visioning is becoming so intoxicating, it is a spiritual high that is better than any drug I have ever experimented with. I had not put 2 and 2 together until afterwards...but that's the beauty of a miracle. It has a way of pleasantly surprising us.

I had a dream where I see a newspaper clipping and can distinctly read the words in the newspaper. The headline reads, "MADONNA WANTS TO MEET THE DREAMER." Supposedly, I am getting married today. I can see people, a lot of people waving and cheering at me. It looks like people are at a New Year's Day celebration and they are crowded along my bedside.

I realized Mom is my Virgin Mary and the beauty I saw in the vision was the innate quality of all mothers to reflect in their eyes the love of our Heavenly Mother. It is awesome to think I may be known as The Dreamer in the heavenly circles and that my Heavenly Mother would send me this personal message to let me know that she wants to make her presence known to me. I know it was truly her because of the synchronicity with which the revelation unfolded. I am humbled and honored. But this miracle did not end here.

Hollywood Wants to Make a Movie Out of My Book

This dream was very powerful. I woke up in the middle of the night quite suddenly out of a deep sleep with the thought, "OH MY GOD, they are making a movie out of my book. They are making a movie out of my book, I can't believe it." I looked over to the end table for my voice recorder so as to not forget the names of the actors, but it was not there. I had left it downstairs in the basement. The dream had such an urgency associated with it that I got up out of bed and ran downstairs to the basement to get it.

In the dream, I find myself sitting around a large executive boardroom table with various actresses, including Jennifer Aniston, Joy Behar, and Shirley MacLaine. We are all discussing the movie. Madonna is there also but her role in the movie is somehow different. Jennifer and I are apparently very close, as though she is my co-star in the movie. Jennifer offers me a ride on her green bicycle that has metal peacock feathers affixed to the seat of the *bike. As the dream ends everyone around the table unanimously nods their heads in support of the project.*

The dream had a great sense of WOW to it. Something inside was telling me this might very well be a prophetic dream because of all the external confirmations that came to play in it. First there was the vision of The Family Portrait where I saw a radiant woman whom I believed was my mother. The second was the synchronicity of my mother having had a dream the same night about us on the beach. Third, was my mother's suggestion that the radiant woman was probably the Virgin Mary (Madonna). Fourth, was reading the newspaper caption in my dream that read: "MADONNA WANTS TO MEET THE DREAMER," whose timing was strategically revealed. I was convinced I had had a Virgin Mary (Madonna) miracle. I knew it was none other than the Virgin Mary who appeared to me in the vision.

I was so excited about this epiphany I immediately called my sister Grace to share with her my miracle of the Virgin Mary.

God had yet another miracle of incredible proportion waiting for us.

"Grace, Grace, you won't believe it......"

Faith and the Virgin Mary Save My Sister's Life

I was on such a spiritual high today I could barely contain myself. Before I left work I called Grace and left her a message to call me first thing because more of the miracle was unfolding. Later that night Grace called me back and I shared everything with her about the dream that I had recorded and completely forgotten about. I told her I had a bit of free time during lunch today and decided to get caught up on some of the dreams that I had dictated and not yet journaled. I told her I put on my headphones and turned on the voice recorder, and the first thing I heard were my words, "I see a newspaper clipping where the headline reads, 'Madonna Wants to Meet the Dreamer.'" I told her I was beside myself.

Could it be that my mother was correct all along in saying that the image of the radiant woman was in fact the Virgin Mary? Holy Potamus!! Talk about a big idea. This was huge!! We sat there on the phone in total awe with each other as though our eyes had truly beheld the image of the Virgin Mary herself. "Could this truly be? Is the Virgin Mary revealing herself to me, to us and the world? Am I truly the carrier of this message? Am I The Dreamer, The Aquarian in the Age of Aquarius, who stands at the door and says to the world, 'Behold the Narrow Gate, enter into the Promised Land, follow your dreams?'"

Grace asked me if she could confess something to me that she had been holding on to for many years. She said she had been trying to be a good person and do the right thing but that it had been hard. She felt that since I came clean to her about my addictions and exposed those things that were haunting me that she too would take this opportunity to expose the skeletons in her closet. I told her that I had been taught to admit to God, myself and another human being the exact nature of my wrongs. I suggested that this, combined with faith, could set her free. She mentioned that she did not know when her number would be called and she did not want to leave this earth unprepared. She felt that with all that had been happening between us and in the world, she wanted to take this opportunity to right her wrongs.

We thought about those who died on 9/11 and during hurricanes Katrina and Rita.

She began to cry as she shared with me the wrongs she had done in the past. I told her to believe that she was now free. I told her about the many places I had read in scripture where Christ healed the sick and forgave people's sins. He said, "Go forth and sin no more." I told her to release her guilt and do as Christ said and sin no more. Be the best person you can be and always hold true to the fruits of the spirit.

Suddenly Grace went silent and all I could hear was what sounded like someone dragging a large heavy dining room table across a wooden floor. I yelled, "Grace, Grace are you there?!" I listened carefully for a few seconds. The sound I heard was not a table but the rhythmic sound of labored breathing. Grace was alone in her apartment and choking. Desperation came over me. "G-R-A-C-E-!!" For a second I did not know what to do. I could not hang up the house phone and call 911 on my cell phone because my cell phone never gets a reliable signal in the house. I did not know her address in Ohio by memory so I would have to log into my computer, which was in the basement, to access my online phone book. I did not have much time to save my sister's life. "G-R-A-C-E-!!" I closed my eyes and all I could do was pray. I needed a miracle now. I held the phone to my heart and from my silent prayer I heard a still small gentle voice say, "*It is okay*...I'm okay, I'm okay." Somehow she had managed to clear her passageway.

She too was given a second chance at life to make things right and make a different in the world. It was a miracle. Our faith in the Virgin Mary saved my sister's life.

Bio Balls and Systems Thinking

This morning I woke up and tried to recall my dream but had difficulty remembering. I had a few minutes before I needed to get out of bed so I laid there and meditated on what my dream might have been about. Suddenly I saw a calligraphic handwritten note in my mind's eye. It was unmistakably written in

English. I looked at the writing carefully to see if I could determine what it was about. I meditated deeper. I could clearly see it was a letter I had written to myself at some point in human history. Suddenly, with a subliminal flash upon the screen of my mind's eye, the word "thinking" appeared superimposed upon the written words. It then slowly vanished. It felt as though I had fallen asleep with a manuscript covering my face. I clearly saw the word "thinking" pressed up against my inner forehead. I then read the sentences immediately in front of me from the original message. The text alluded to all of the great thinkers of the world and some common shared purpose.

I was still half asleep and thought I could never remember all this written material. It did not even occur to me to get out my voice recorder because this did not feel like a dream.

While in deep thought, I recalled the details of the dream.

In the dream, I can see my third eye cast upon the heavens and within the pupil of this eye stands the great elephant Ganesh. As he stands inside the pupil, the great Ganesh peers out at me. I can see his trunk, ears and head sway from side to side as he motions for me to follow him. He then turns and retreats back deep within the pupil of my eye. My consciousness goes forth to follow him. As I enter, I gain form and find myself standing naked in a place where everything around me is white. Radiant white light fills this inner space.

As I turn to observe my surroundings, I notice I am standing upon a soft bed of pure white Styrofoam peanuts. Puzzled at the somewhat awkward situation in which I find myself, I look down at the peanuts and notice that not all of them are really peanuts. Some are hollow white bio balls similar to those used in aquarium filtration systems. I move one of the bio balls with my big toe to examine it from a distance. The ball splits open into two equal halves. The lines on the bio ball remind me of the latitude and longitude lines upon our globe.

It's a Miracle; High on Life

On my way in to work I was pondering the meaning of the Styrofoam peanuts and the calligraphic note when something caught my eye. It appeared someone had sprayed some type of white foam or shaving cream all along the sidewalk and shrubs lining the street where I walked. For three blocks, as I continued walking, this mysterious foam was everywhere -- in the trees, on the shrubs, along the street, in the gutter -- it was everywhere. With curiosity piqued, I walked over to a secluded area to examine the foam more closely. Not wanting anyone to see me, I inconspicuously moved the foam with the toe of my shoe. A sudden wave of eeriness ran through me as remembrance of the dream came rushing back. They were sticky white foam peanuts.

I continued down the path. As I waited for the light to change to cross the street, there upon the ground was a shiny penny. I knew this all had to have some hidden meaning, for this was not a sheer coincidence. Unclear as to the meaning of the events that were unfolding, I decided to meditate for a few minutes when I got to work. I said a few prayers and sat quietly behind my desk. I then had a vision where I saw a woman who walked up to me. She had glistening golden hair and stood with her hands behind her back. Smiling, she stood there and quietly looked at me. She then brought her hand from around her back and in her hand she held a beautiful red rose with a golden stem. She offered it to me with the words, "I love you."

My dream had come true.

High on Crystal Light

Last night I had a dream. In the dream, I am with a group of friends huddled around a campfire smoking Crystal Light out of a clear see-through glass peace pipe that is shaped just like my voice recorder. The smoke from the glass pipe is so good when inhaled that I do not want to stop smoking it.

Actually, now that I think about it, my voice recorder is shaped like a cigar. At one point, I woke up and felt I was being forced out of the dream, pushed out and being told to go home.

"Go home. Stop smoking up all our Crystal Light."

"Wait, wait just give me one more puff of that Crystal Light."

I guess they let me back into their circle because now I am taking another drag off the glass pipe. Every time I inhale I feel an intense exaltation. Thinking I want to take some of this Crystal Light back with me, I conveniently place the pipe in my night stand drawer when no one is looking.

Everyone is now looking around the camp asking, *"What happened to the Crystal Light?"*

"I don't know."

After everyone leaves, I reach back in my night stand drawer to grab the glass pipe. I look at the glass pipe and there is plenty of Crystal Light left in it for me to enjoy. Needless to say, I do not want to wake up this morning.

I woke up to the words of the song *"This is Your Life,"* by Switchfoot, playing in my head. I meditated on the words to this song. This IS my life and YES, I have become who I want to be, living life for the Glory of God. How beautiful it is to be at ONE. I am a miracle.

Murder She Wrote – The Natural High

IT'S A MIRACLE; HIGH ON LIFE

This dream reminded me of an episode from *"Murder She Wrote."* There was a guy who had his throat slashed. Afterward, they played the scenes back and you found out how the murder was committed. Things you did not notice the first time became apparent the second time.

My friend Curtis has a bag filled with thick chunks of oranges and apples that have been peeled and cut into small pieces. He seasons the fruit with crystals and puts it in the plastic bag. The crystals melt and are absorbed by the fruit. He then eats the fruit and goes out dancing. He experiences a natural high produced by ingesting the fruit.

Curtis has a movie club card that allows him various member privileges. He rents a movie that is part of a three box set trilogy. The trilogy is considered a classic.

I can see the writing on the box set. It is written in a fancy italicized calligraphy. They are really good movies and one of them is this "Murder She Wrote" episode. I act as though I do not want to see it because I really was not invited to share in the oranges. I have seen parts of the movie trilogy so I know it is a really good movie series.

I tell Curtis I do not want to go to the party. I stay home and quietly eat some of the leftover oranges and watch the movie after Curtis and his friends have all left. I start feeling this wonderful sensation associated with the natural high induced by the crystallized oranges. The movie is very good. At the end, they show us how the murder was committed by giving us the special member privileged inside scoop, the behind the scenes clips associated with being a movie club card member.

I am high on life today. I live an enchanted life. It is a natural high that comes from all the little synchronicities and miracles born of the fruits of the spirit. The Bible says in Gal 5:22: "But the fruit of the Spirit is love, joy, peace, patience, kindness, goodness, faithfulness, gentleness and self-control."

IN THE COURSE OF A DREAM EMANUEL FOR LOVE

God is inviting me to discover a new substance stored deep within me that is a natural high. These synchronistic miracles do provide an indescribable natural euphoria. The movie is my life, my dreams and my meditative visions viewed through the eyes of one who has an appreciation and love for the one true classic *"Murder She Wrote."* In Jesus' death I have come to know that I am not the physical body. It is through his eyes that I have come to realize I AM that I AM.

We Got Rid of The Skunk! Elixirs for All!

I had a dream. There is a skunk in a display case that I am helping get rid of. The display case is sealed so I am not affected by the smell of the skunk. The skunk is agitated and sprays the window of the display case. We think this might be a safe time to grab it and throw it out into the wild where it belongs. We had tried to remove it from the house previously but it kept running back into the house. Every time we put it out, it would run back into the house in fear. It had taken refuge in the house for so long that its normal inclination was to run back in the house every time.

We finally have an idea to squeeze the little guy's neck to keep him from spraying long enough to carry him deep into the nearby woods where he will hopefully not be able to find his way back. We decide to go with the plan. We believe we are successful this time in ridding ourselves of our skunk problem. We then celebrate by enjoying an elixir that is so intoxicating it makes me feel incredibly wonderful. I am warm and fuzzy inside.

I woke up in the middle of the night after having drunk the elixir and boy, I felt so incredibly high. "WOW! That was SO GOOD!" I looked around my bedroom and thought to myself, "I want more of that."

IT'S A MIRACLE; HIGH ON LIFE

I laid back down and began meditating. I quickly entered a full dream state while still fully awake where I found myself deep in space on the bridge of a spacecraft. I was looking out the windows of the spacecraft and admiring how beautiful the universe looked from this new vantage point. The people aboard this ship were honored observers witnessing a spectacular part of our galaxy. Everyone aboard the ship had a unique skill and responsibility and they were highly respected in their line of work. No one questioned the authority of another. Everyone worked in harmony as a team.

The dream vision faded and I opened my eyes to find a faerie hovering over my bed. He had pale blue markings on his cheeks like whiskers with a pointy nose on his face. He reminded me of a little Indian boy. He was so cute and colorful. He looked upon me with loving eyes and said, "Thank you for setting me free."

There is no separation between us and anything else. We are in all places and in all things. Everything has its purpose. We all have a little skunk inside us we call the ego who is entrapped by fear. Our spirit cannot be adversely affected in any way by the ego. Like children under a loving parent, we are protected from harm to ourselves. We must escort our warm and fuzzy friend deep within, to come out on the other side transformed into a God-aware spiritual being who no longer lives in the shadow but is now part of the ONE, integrated whole within himself. Nothing exists apart from God. We can truly say, "I am free."

The Land of Canaan

"1 For the kingdom of heaven is like unto a man that is a householder, which went out early in the morning to hire laborers into his vineyard.

2 And when he had agreed with the laborers for a penny a day, he sent them into his vineyard

9 And when they came that were hired about the eleventh hour, they received every man a penny." (Matthew 20:1-2 20:9KJV)

He is One of Us; God Brings Forth a Love Beetle

On this night, I woke up in the middle of the night with a sudden urge to go to the bathroom. I turned to look at my digital alarm clock and the time was 4:25am. I got up, did my business, and returned to bed. Preconditioned, I closed my eyes and began meditating. I immediately fell into a Wakefully Induced Lucid Dream state. Being half asleep, my altered state did not immediately register with me. I saw before me a video screen upon which was playing what seemed to be a car commercial. They were driving the car along a mountainous terrain to demonstrate the superb handling of the vehicle during aggressive turns.

They then drove the car on the highway to contrast with the smooth ride of the open road. Instead of focusing my mind on the car, my mind was captivated by the beautiful scenery through which the car was traveling. "I'll bet you this is where my dreams come up with the vibrant colors to paint pictures in my mind," I thought. That was when my brain clicked. "You ARE dreaming! How could you be watching a television commercial at 4:25am if you never watch television? Don't you remember you just came from the bathroom? Pay attention, you are dreaming!" Knowing this, I became fully lucid as I observed where the dream vision was taking me.

The final caption of the commercial read: "JOSEPH JURIST; HE IS ONE OF US." My mind screamed, "What! You woke me up for this?" That scream disrupted my mind's television signal. I opened my eyes thinking, "What was that all about?" A little voice inside me said, "You had better not pass judgment too prematurely. Go back inside to see what you might discover about yourself."

I closed my eyes once again, relaxed and returned to my meditation to try to recover the signal. The signal soon came back with the words: "JOSEPH IS YOUR PARTNER IN LOVE AND SEX." The signal then faded and all I could see around me was my bedroom exactly as I had left it in my waking life. In the hallway outside my bedroom walked a man. Frightened, I opened my eyes and looked toward my bedroom door that leads to the hallway. At that moment, a man in spirit walked into my bedroom and came up alongside my bed.

I immediately affirmed, "I am not afraid. God is with me." The man held his hands clasped in front of him and was radiating the colors of blue and red from within the area about his waist. He then extended his arm out toward me as if to hand me something. I thought, "NO, NO; I'm not taking anything from you unless I know who you are." I crouched back into my covers and hid my hands. He reached over with his right hand and grabbed my left wrist to open my palm. I felt a static shock the moment our hands touched.

Thinking I had no choice but to accept what this man had for me, I said, "OK, what is it you have for me?" He then opened his left hand in which he held a yo-yo. He then began playing with the yo-yo. The yo-yo would go down, spin and come back up; down, spin and come back up. The center of the yo-yo had an inner red glow. He spun his yo-yo three times and placed it in the palm of my left hand and vanished.

I laid back down with my new yo-yo in hand and returned to my meditation. I somehow knew exactly what he meant to say in delivering this gift.

I am the yo-yo spinning in time, the ambigram, the third dimensional reality in which I exist, tethered by a string to the hand of God, the Holy Spirit, and my Higher Self. I am in God's hand. Tethered to my Divine Self, I can never stray far from the hand of God. I remain forever within His presence. I can safely experience time with the curiosity of a child, as that is how I find myself. I now hold my life and essence in the palm of my hand, in full awareness of my I AM Presence. I am the Dreamer and creator of my reality, my own judge and jurist. I am one in spirit and an inalienable part of the Universal Mind of God.

As I laid there pondering the meaning of what I had just experienced, I had a vision. I saw before me an ominous billowing of clouds as if a storm was approaching. The clouds began to take form; something was beginning to come though. It was the face of GOD. So powerful and great was this man's face impressed upon the clouds that I could hardly breathe. I looked and marveled at the majesty my eyes beheld, when from his right eye, as a tear drop, came forth an iridescent green beetle.

When I arrived at work in the morning, I quickly looked up the significance of beetles. I pulled up my trusty Wikipedia and on its page for beetles I scrolled down and found an incredibly beautiful green beetle very similar to the one I saw in my vision. The caption below the picture read:

"Striped Love Beetle *Eudicella Gralli* from the forests of Central Africa. The iridescent wing cases are used in marriage ceremonies."

How interesting that this green beetle could be a symbol for love and marriage and that it came forth from the eye of God. I also learned that through the development stages of a beetle's life it undergoes a metamorphosis much like that of a butterfly as it matures into an adult. I feel I too have undergone a metamorphosis. I can only hope to be as beautiful as the green beetle that walked across the face of God, my beloved creator upon whose soul I rest.

A Plan for Salvation

I had a dream that I was flying above a small Hawaiian island. I can see the lay of the bay and the water below. It is so beautiful, so crystal clear. Suddenly a very large tsunami is seen on the horizon coming our way. I can see the ocean rising in the distance. The wave will soon hit the mainland.

The ferries running between the mainland and the little islands are running normally, unbeknownst of what is to come. Suddenly the wave hits and many people are affected and now they are scurrying to return to the mainland. I too want to depart and leave all my clothing behind.

We soon find out that there is a plan in place to save the distressed victims. They come in with large ships that can ferry people back to the mainland.

Leaving my clothes and all my possessions behind, I board one of the ships. I room with a good looking young man who is in the military. He has managed to escape with just a white bath robe. He befriends me. In fear we sleep in a cabin huddled together more to ease my fear than his.

At one point his robe falls to his side exposing the profile of his waist. The curves and details of his waist are so beautiful it reminds me of the painting by Michelangelo where the man is reaching up to heaven to touch the hand of God. There was beauty to his nakedness.

There is most certainly a plan for salvation. There are a host of preparations being made to guarantee a safe return to the mainland. My help has come from my many angels, faeries and spirit guides. We need only reach out our hand and earnestly ask for help and God will answer by summoning his many faithful servants to the task, to sleep with us where necessary. We need only come as we are. We need not fear the help when it arrives. God is so much more powerful and great than any shadows that might cross our path. There is nothing to fear when we rest in the arms of God.

A Delayed Harvest Moon

I had a dream that I am a college student at Catholic University and my brother Paz is coming to visit me. Eager to meet with my brother, I wake up early and leave my dorm room to meet him on the other side of campus. On my way there, it occurs to me that it would have been wise to have confirmed that my brother was in fact coming before heading out this morning.

I call my brother Paz who tells me he has not intended on coming today but now that I am expecting him, he will arrange to come. I am frustrated now with the delay, because I could have made better use of my time. I do not want to go back home to wait for him again. Alas, I surrender.

I woke up a minute before my alarm clock sounded. I quickly hit the snooze button and began my ritual meditation. I closed my eyes and on the screen of my inner eye, I saw a large tree with beautiful fall foliage whose leaves were red and yellow. The tree was set in front of a huge harvest moon that spanned the entire tree. It was as if the leaves were illuminated from behind by the light of the moon.

I wanted to see the source of the moon's light but the moon was obscured by the fall leaves. The leaves themselves were dazzling in color.

I then saw a mighty flowing river which reflected the fall colors. I walked along the river to where it met a placid lake that reflected nothing but the sky above. The scene was so beautiful that I was overtaken by an incredible sense of peace.

This is the best time in human history because we are poised to receive the harvest. The grapes are ready and the time is now. It is in surrender to the inward path that the waters of the lake become placid to reflect the glory of God within. It is a time when every man receives his penny, for the harvest is good.

The second coming of Christ is something we will experience on the inside. It is very real and not something that is imaginary. It is delayed for those who choose not to invest the time on the inward path. Let those who have eyes see and let those who have ears hear. We are the fruit of the vine. The season is now. The tables are set for those who hear the invitation. Come one come all.

Joe Camel Speaks: Hidden Messages

Last night I had a dream where I am hoarding cigarettes, lots of them. They are like those small travel bars of soap that people take from hotel rooms. I had collected these

The Land of Canaan

cigarettes over time and now I have a whole bunch stashed away. I am traveling and for some reason, I decide to take them all with me even though I know it is best to leave them at home.

I am walking through an airport security check and my intuition tells me that I am going to be stopped, pulled aside and questioned about all the cigarettes. There is no way anyone is not going to notice the cigarettes stuffed in my pockets. It is too late to turn back because that would surely arouse even more suspicion so I decide to take a chance and go with it. Through some miracle, I somehow make it through the checkpoint without being noticed. Now at my destination, I have the problem of getting the cigarettes back home. I do not even smoke but for some reason I want them just in case I ever decide I want to start smoking.

My alarm rang and I hit the snooze button and began my ritual meditation. I was lying there with my eyes closed yet fully awake when in my minds eye I saw a full screen video as if I had just walked into a movie theatre. On the big screen was a really cool guy, very tanned and slightly sunburned. Even though he looked to be in his early 40's, his hair was completely white. He had a very thick head of hair. He reclined slightly to enjoy a cigarette. He wore a blue winter scarf around his neck, a white shirt and red pants. The contrast in colors made him look somewhat cartoonish. It reminded me of one of the old Joe Camel cigarette commercials.

He smiled wide to reveal his pearly white teeth. As the light hit his teeth it cast shadows upon the enamel. I then noticed a hidden message worked into the shadows upon his teeth. It was a set of numbers: 177. It felt like one of those children's puzzles where you try to find the hidden images.

My alarm went off again and I opened my eyes to hit snooze and noticed that the time read: 7:01am. I thought, "That's a coincidence." I then returned to my meditation wanting to see more. I then started having a vision of the Greek God Pan; half-man half-goat. He was running, except this time he too was smoking and wearing a scarf around his neck. I could see cartoon-style clouds in the sky as he ran off to the left.

After running for a while he stopped and transformed into a man. He then walked a little distance, found a horse and got on the horse and rode off into the sunset.

My alarm clock rang again. I looked at the clock. The time was now 7:10 am. It left me with a very weird feeling.

Intrigued by the hidden message in my WILD state, I decided to do a search on Wikipedia for Joe Camel to see what I might learn, since the imagery was very similar. I pulled up the page on Joe Camel and read it. Nothing seemed to hit me at first until I read that Joe Camel ads had controversial hidden imagery that was sexually suggestive. Ironically, the hidden imagery in the Camel ads centered around the Camel's mouth. I could not believe the similarities. I never knew anything about the hidden images in the Camel ads. I was never a cigarette smoker. How did I know this? All I remembered was that the Camel was popular with kids.

Dreams are jam-packed with hidden messages and nothing is ever quite what it appears to be on the surface. They teach us to think out of the box and are integral to the process of creating our physical reality. There is truth to be found at every level. We must remove all notions upon which we have come to base the world around us. We must become child-like. Dreams are fluid. They move with you. They are the roots of the matrix in which we create our physical reality.

THE LAND OF CANAAN

In the end, we find that all things hold truth. Our infinite wisdom lies just below the surface. It should not be overlooked. To do so is to overlook humanity's potential toward achieving Cosmic Consciousness. Within our One Mind is the true Christ Consciousness that is our birthright as the child of God that we are. It is our sole purpose -- to be and live our lives in true and utter bliss in full awareness of our I AM Self.

The Multi-Dimensional Ouiji Board

I had a dream where I go back in time. Joe, my partner at the time, is acting very mysterious. It feels like he is avoiding me to entertain himself.

I find that I have tied up my bicycle outside the house and left my book bag on top of the trash can. I fear someone might have seen my book bag and accessed my things. I need to be more careful not to leave my things out in the open.

I go back in the house unexpectedly and discover there are other people in our house. Joe had told me he was not messing around. This proves to me that he is in fact hiding something from me. There is a woman on the sofa sitting down and her blouse is slightly unbuttoned in a very provocative way. I look at her and ask her what she is doing in my house. She looks at me with a hand gesture that tells me, "Isn't it obvious?"

There are several other people in the house. Joe finally admits that there is more to his life than meets the eye. I feel he is still withholding information. I want to know what is going on.

"This is my house and you are my lover."

He is lying on the ground in total ecstasy. I am getting frustrated because I want to know who or what is pleasuring him. I casually reach under his belly and into his groin to see if he secretly has someone under him. He lifts his body and I can see a hole that looks like the mouth of an anemone. I assume he has his member in the mouth of the anemone.

I then stick my finger in the hole to prove it for myself. My finger goes deep into the hole. I ask him to explain this "wormhole." He is in total ecstasy and is not saying anything; he is not doing anything. He simply remains perfectly still. Others are around him, in my house, who are also in this same state of total ecstasy. It is a mind game. Everyone is ecstatic except me.

I tell him I want to know what is going on. I am then shown a computer program that appears on a screen. The program is incredibly vibrant and colorful. It reminds me of an Ouija Board with many abstract symbols, letters and numbers. I am afraid of it because I have been taught to stay away from things like this. I know I cannot allow my instilled fears to stop me from knowing the truth. I have to get to the bottom of this and figure out what is going on here. I want to know what they know. I want to know the mystery of life and I believe the computer program holds the key.

I become aware that the selections on the board respond to my thoughts. I begin activating a few of the symbols to observe their effects. The program suddenly creates a virtual void space. Instantly, geometric shapes and cubes of all kinds, along with other multi-dimensional shapes appear suspended within the virtual space. A three dimensional rectangle appears with a depth of about one inch. It pivots on one of its corners and comes to rest on its end.

I realize I am now able to perceive things with multi-dimensional vision and what I am looking at is the system command console. The console contains all patterns, letters and symbols. I see the text "TXO." I realize we are all multi-dimensional beings and the people I see in my house are from other dimensions. They are as close to us as we are to ourselves yet they are not of or in this world.

I can be fully engaged with them through this portal and nobody else would ever know who I am communicating with because they are from other dimensions. They are a part of me.

The Land of Canaan

We carry this wormhole portal within us wherever we go. That portal or doorway is our third eye or Christ Consciousness. The computer program creates the alignment and key that enables us to enter the portal.

I am a little jealous because Joe seems to prefer this wormhole over me. He finally admits that he has had an intimate relationship with these people for a very long time. This wormhole through which he inserts his member, his life force, is like a drug. He tells me there is nothing to fear.

I then see God seated in a large armchair with all of us around him and he is showing us how the portal is accessed through our Higher Self. He pulls out an umbrella and opens it and spins it on its axis. We cannot see Him but we know He IS. He stands just beyond a thin veil that separates us from him.

This dream was a treasure store of age-old wisdom recovered. The truth is plain and simple. Feel it, move with it and become one with it. It is your partner, embrace it. Judge it not, for in judging, you judge yourself.

It is through consciously activating the dream symbols through the power of lucid dreaming and lucid living that we achieve purposeful manifestation. That is, manifestation that is guided by our true inner purpose; a purpose-filled life. Our highest dreams are made manifest. We all have this Ouiji Board within us that serves not only to provide the answers we seek but also the means to create those circumstances in our lives that will help bring about our purpose. It is where our true power to create lies.

Our trash is everybody's business. In heaven there is nothing to hide, for nothing can be hidden. We have a limited view of things and therefore we need to seek our own inner guidance. The obvious to spirit is not always obvious to me. Don't let your fears and your preconceived notions keep you from knowing the truth.

Burning Bush Photographer

I had a dream where I am being photographed by a professional photographer. He wants me to wear a thick black robe. He tells me that he is unable to get a good picture of me because I emanate too much light. There are streaks of light showing in the exposed picture. I look at the robe he has placed on me that I am now wearing and I can see zebra-like streaks on my robe.

Unable to believe it, I look into the lens of the camera and I see the image he has captured. I see myself, or who I am told I am, seated Indian style in the middle of the room. All I can see in the image is a big ball of light emanating from my solar plexus. The light is so intense I cannot see my body or face. All I can see of me are my legs in meditation seated Indian style.

What is Producing the Light?

I then had a second dream where I am lying in my bed with another guy conversing about life. A flame is sparked and the sheets of my bed catch fire. I try to put the fire out with a fire extinguisher. There is barely enough to douse the flame. The sheets are smoldering.

I suddenly awoke and looked around the room. The room was filled with an intense red light and there was smoke rising from the bright red hue beneath and around my bed. Although I saw the smoke, I could not smell anything burning. I looked up at the vents in my bedroom and it seemed that smoke was coming in through the vents.

In my house I have two separate smoke detector systems, a primary and a backup. Neither system had tripped.

I came to the conclusion I must have carried over the smoke from the dream world I had just left.

The purpose of dreams is to help us transform the mortal body into a body of light, a light being, by reuniting us with our twin flame, the spark of divinity within, that voice of the Holy Spirit as spoken through the eyes of our beloved Higher Self. In the moment we see ourselves through the eyes of the Holy Spirit we realize our true divinity. We are multi-dimensional beings.

You can see it for yourself. You come into your own awareness. Your essence is pure Light, whose source is Love.

In My Fathers House There Are Big Aquariums

I had a dream where I am shown what negative images are. They show me a cellophane sheet that is reflective. The surface of the cellophane reflects only the positive image. All negative images do not reflect. I can see the people around me but when I look into the mirror the people are not reflected back because their bodies are cast in negative images. This is not negative in a bad sense but more like a yin / yang of opposing polarities.

They back me into a corner and place the cellophane in front of me so that I can see that I have no reflection, yet I know I am there. I can see myself and those around me but none of us cast a reflection in the cellophane. I can see that when the soft pliable cellophane vibrates or moves the creases or folds conduct the light like fiber optic strands.

In the Course of a Dream Emanuel for Love

They then bring me to a body of water, a lake, where they show me that there is no reflection in the surface of the water. I am told I am in spirit.

Next they take me to travel along a residential city street where we are floating about five feet above the surface of the earth like ghosts. We are passing alongside some children who are riding their bicycles. We watch them play. Then as the kids come close, they sense our presence yet they cannot see exactly where we are standing.

I woke up and grabbed my voice recorder to record the details of the dream. I then closed my eyes to meditate. While fully conscious, I found myself in what appeared to be the void of space without a body hovering above what looked like a small spaceship the size of a small house that was in orbit around a celestial body. I was pure consciousness. The spaceship was absolutely stunningly beautiful. It was a ship of light. I had never seen anything like it in my life. It appeared to be cloaked because it had a translucent shell but I could definitely see the curvatures in the body of the ship. It conducted light impulses of many colors. I was mesmerized by the lights and had an extreme sense of inner peace.

There was no way I was going to allow myself to slip back into a deep sleep. I continued to meditate while remaining fully conscious. Everything suddenly shifted and I found myself in and among moonstruck images. I was now one of them in their virtual space. They were as real as I am. I was in their dimension.

Everything was yellow and black. The moonstruck figures were ice skating on a lake that had many boulders that protruded up out of the water. The surface of the water was shimmering like deep yellow colored mercury. It was so clear and beautiful that I could not believe my eyes. Life was so simple and carefree there. It was so utterly amazing, beautiful and peaceful.

"Where is this all coming from?" I thought.

The moonstruck images were extremely jubilant, gliding gracefully just above the surface of the water. Every once in a while I would see their feet glide against the ripples of the water, which caused a spray like that of jet skis.

"Oh my God this is so beautiful." I opened my eyes to pinch myself to make sure I was actually conscious. I was definitely still awake. I grabbed my voice recorder again to record the details.

I returned to meditate and again found myself as one of the ice skaters gliding upon this beautiful yellow lake. Free, free, free I was. "How do I know how to skate in this manner?" I pondered. Grace came perfectly natural to me. I lost myself in the sheer joy and bliss that was to be found here. It went on forever.

I finally felt myself beginning to drift off into sleep but held on to consciousness and dragged it with me. I was determined to experience this fully awake; all of it. I wanted to know what it was to Live the Dream. I found that, depending on my level of concentration, I could slip in and out of different realms and dimensions. I began having visions of spirits whom I did not know but who apparently knew me. I did not want to lose the signal so I remained calm and motionless. They were talking to me telepathically. I did not want to stop to record the details for fear I would not be able to return.

I was inundated with information like a computer processing a download. My inner vision then went blank with a bluish lavender colored screen in front of my mind's eye. Even though I was not seeing anything with my physical eyes, or my mind's eye, my brain was experiencing perfect images on a non-visual level as if I were receiving a direct feed from Source. It was utterly amazing to see without seeing. It was like intuitively watching a movie and being able to see it fully without the use of sight. This had to be the ultimate visual effect for a clairsentient.

I quickly became disoriented, not knowing who I really was. I seemed to become the characters in the dream. The non-visual part of the dream went like this:

I am working for an older man who has many aquariums in his house, both fresh water and salt water, much like the ones I have in my waking life. The fish in the aquariums are huge and I do mean huge. The aquariums are so large he is able to keep entire sets of schooling fish. The fish are silver with red fins. They looked like a cross between a silver dollar fish and a tin foil barb. In another tank he has blue catfish with wings, flying fish of sorts whose wings are tissue thin. These flying fish swim like brine shrimp. As a matter of fact, they also have whiskers like male brine shrimp, that crown the tops of their heads. They are the most beautiful of all the creatures of the sea. I want to take one home with me to add to my salt water tank.

The largest of the blue catfish appears to have died already. I am saddened because it was the most beautiful and the largest of the blue winged catfish. Unable to find the owner of the house to ask him for permission to take one home, I run back to my house to tell my father about the wonderful job I now have working for the man up the street who owns the big house with all the aquariums.

My father looks at me and asks me, "Son, do they look like these?" Behind my father are mirror images, identical replicas of the aquariums in the house I had just come from. He throws me into confusion. "WHAT?" I feel I am straddling two dimensions or realities. I tell him, "No father, the man has one fish in particular that is super large. It is the most beautiful fish in the sea." I turn my head back and point in the direction of the old man's house. I point to the fish, the biggest fish in the aquarium, who is now swimming away from me. My father then says to me, "Is it not this one?" To which he points to an equally large fish in his tank. It is identical.

I realize this is all a mirrored illusion and actually the same house of the man I work for. The man I work for is my father and I am in my father's house. I cannot believe what is happening to me. I feel like I am seeing myself for who I truly am and in so doing I behold the image of my father.

I opened my eyes and recorded the details of the dream. This was awesome! I believe one of the greatest joys God has is watching us in our naiveté discover who we really are. Our joy comes in reading between the lines. I have found Christ and I have seen angels, though I may not have known it when I saw them, as my child mind described them otherwise. Yet I do know today that I need not go far, for it is all found within me.

Enter Canaan and Leave Your Earthly Wings at the Door

Yesterday marked a new beginning in my life. I let go of the last major vice that I felt was keeping me tied to the physical plane and preventing me from moving forward on my spiritual path. It will suffice to say, it was a collection of movies that I had accumulated over the years and were now stashed in my closet that did not serve to build and uplift my spirit. I felt I must rid myself of them and now was the perfect time to finally make the decision because the trash trucks were due to roll through first thing in the morning.

These things were a part of the old me. It was not enough to say I just will not watch them because then why have them? A time comes when we have

In the Course of a Dream Emanuel for Love

to purge the old to make room for the new. My spirit wants to do the right thing in all areas of my life. I want to be able to be free to fully taste the milk and honey without having to drag this yoke around. I have also come to know that for everything in faith that I give up, I gain ten-fold by way of the joy and bliss that comes from being spiritually connected. Miracles are just a byproduct of doing everything you do for the glory of God and in service to others.

The blessing I received from releasing this yoke would turn out to be incredible. Here is how it went. I did my usual prayers and meditation and drifted off into dreamland.

I had a dream where I am having an argument with Joe, my ex, where I am telling him I can no longer accept him and his things in my life or in my house. He is outside my bedroom insisting I let him back into the bedroom. I keep telling him I am just not having it anymore. I have made my decision.

In defiance, he says he is coming back in and is going to do anything he so chooses whether I like it or not. He then storms into the bedroom but instead of it being Joe who comes in, it is a group of dark spirits. To protect myself, I send forth from my being waves of rainbow colored light. I can see the waves knock the dark spirits off balance. The dark spirits keep sending in more reinforcements to try to intimidate me and tear at my determination. Eventually it becomes more than I can bear and the last dark spirit comes charging at me with great impact, which wakes me right up out of bed.

I opened my eyes and floating above me was the dark spirit of a woman in her 40's with salt and pepper hair. Interestingly enough she was completely dark except for her grey hair. Knowing she was the one who had rammed me and woke me up, I refused to let my fear get the best of me. We locked eyes. She knew I could see her and I was not backing down. She circled me, never taking her eyes off me. I took a deep breath and said, "This is it. NO MORE." Again I visualized my light and the light of the universe going out of my being to her. She began to back off and I could see terror in her eyes. She was now afraid of me. With that, she fled and as she fled dozens of dark spirits fled with her like the scattering of black field mice.

Wow, I could not believe what had just happened. Who have I allowed to take room in my house? I then laid my head back down on my pillow and out of the corner of my eye I could see golden light glistening beside me. I turned and it was the face of Jennifer, my guardian angel. Her golden hair was the source of the golden light I had seen out of the corner of my eye. She had been the one to save me and cast out the demons from my room. Our eyes met and she knew I could see her. Her face then slowly vanished and I closed my eyes and meditated on the rainbow lights that surrounded me.

As I sank deeper into meditation, the rainbow lights turned into a field of petals in a lush green garden filled with trees and flowers of every color possible. There was a river of blue petals that flowed through the garden. It reminded me of one of the floats at the Rose Parade. The garden was ablaze with rainbow colors. I heard a voice say, "This is the Land of Canaan." I then understood why it was called a land flowing with milk and honey. I saw what looked like a bird walking upon a meadow. It was a large bird the size of a hen or possibly a partridge. It was a beautiful bird and as it walked by it turned and looked me in the eye, acknowledging my presence. It had no fear of my presence in the garden.

I drifted further into a deep sleep. I was now seeing moonstruck figures but instead of people I saw two bears in love. They were affectionately playing with each other. It was so playful and cute I fell right to sleep.

I then had a dream where I am seeing these people who are shape shifters. They are at war with each other. They are constantly shooting at each other and even killing each other. They are so engrossed in their feud that they have failed to realize that as soon as they shoot and kill someone of the opposition, that person quickly undergoes a shape shift and reappears directly behind the person that has attacked and killed him. There is no running from the crime. It is a self-perpetuating, never ending vicious cycle. Shooting the person or killing him only allows the person to undergo a shift in shape and change of appearance and return revitalized and recharged. It keeps going and going and going. It is never ending.

I then become lucid and step into the battlefield of the dream. I yell out to them, "What do you think you people are doing?" but no one pays me any attention. They consider me a threat and begin trying to attack me but their bullets have no effect on me. I am somehow protected.

I then had a false awakening. I found myself in my bedroom. One of the persons from the battlefield in my dream was standing beside my bed in spirit. I mentally told him, "Look, I can see you and I was telling you the truth about your little war game." He then suddenly realized I was in fact telling him the truth all along so he dropped his guard and climbed into bed with me.

"What are you doing?" I asked him. "Just because I'm trying to help you see your error doesn't mean you are welcome in my bed."

I reached out my hand and as I did I noticed I could not see my hand. I then waved my hand in front of my face a couple of times and although I could feel my hand passing in front of my face I could not see it. I then realized this was a false awakening.

Not knowing what to expect, I played into the dream and went to grab

The Land of Canaan

the spirit of the man who had climbed into my bed. I did not want to lose sight of where this spirit was since they are translucent and difficult to see and easily blend into their environment and slip away. I reached out to him with my invisible hand and to my surprise I could actually feel his arms.

"What? How is it that I could feel something that is in spirit form?"

I then ran my hand up his shoulders and felt his jaw bone. To my surprise I could feel this person's entire form and it was not mine. He was thin and smooth like a baby. It freaked me out.

"How is it that I can't see him or me but I can feel his body?"

In a sudden confusion he slipped away from my grip. "Where did he go?" I then felt him come up on me from behind. I reached behind me without him knowing that I knew he was there and grabbed hold of his wrist. I jumped out of bed. When I jumped I went flying across the room and landed over by my bedroom door.

In the process I lost hold of the spirit's arm so I turned around and looked over to my bed. I could see my body lying there in bed under the sheets, sleeping alone.

"How weird. Have I died? Where am I?"

I knew there was a mirror in the bedroom hanging on the wall so I walked over to the mirror to see if I could see my reflection. I looked into the mirror from across my bed and did not see my reflection in the mirror. What I did see was the body of a small three-year-old hanging on my back like a backpack, yet I could not see me. The child faced away from the mirror with his head buried in my invisible back and his arms wrapped around and holding onto me. The child had not yet seen himself.

I quietly came in closer to the mirror to see who this child was without startling him. He was cute with curly brown hair just like the pictures of me when I was a child. I thought, "Could that be me; my inner child maybe?" I guess the kid sensed someone was thinking about him so he turned his head and finally caught his own reflection in the mirror.

It was a boy's face that looked like me in a distorted way. He had somewhat of a square instead of oval head. Nevertheless, he was very cute with rosy checks and curly brown hair. I leaned a little closer into the mirror and thought, "He is so cute." My heart felt love and compassion for the child. His face then began to transform into the faces of other children. "Wait a second," I told myself, "Who is this shape shifter attached to my back? Could this kid be reflecting all the childhood faces of my many lifetimes?" I was captivated at the many faces he bore.

Then something interesting began to happen. The distortion of his face became worse and worse with every new face until his teeth were all ugly and decayed and he began to look more like a Quasimodo than a beautiful three-year-old boy. I felt as if he had never gazed into a mirror and was just now experiencing his own reflection. I could see fear set in as his face distorted and he discovered who he really was. He began to shrink in size like the Wicked Witch of the East.

In the light he shrank and withered until his face was so small it vanished completely. I then shook my head and awoke from the dream.

I instantly grabbed my voice recorder to capture every detail of this most incredible out of body experience.

The Land of Canaan

I have to wonder if in our fall from grace we exchanged the wings on our back for an ego on our back.

Fly High Little Proud Bird and Build Your Nest Upon The Highest Cliff

I had a dream that the company I worked for has merged with another firm. Joe has landed and sealed the deal. I am told that I cannot call in sick anymore or I will be fired. This guy I have been working with before is already terminated because he is not much of a producer. We are getting ready to celebrate the merger and acquisition. Jerry is there with another guy who tells me he has heard that Joe has already met someone else and has moved on with his life. It really does not bother me because I accept it for what it is. I am happy with my new life. There is a tiny part of me that is sad that it did not work out between us, but life goes on. I lay my head on my friend Ben's shoulder for support.

I walk out into the courtyard where there are many flowers and trees. "I am now free." With that thought I become a bird and I take flight and fly very high in the sky. I can feel myself flapping my wings and it feels so good to be free. I am now free to build a nest in the cliffs of the mountainside where there are incredible views of the land. I can be proud of myself because I am such a good bird.

This weekend was phenomenal. I loved it. I was on a spiritual high unrivaled to anything I have ever felt in my entire life. I was on an "AH HA" of global proportions. I could not contain my joy.

To sit in total rapture is incredible. I cannot kid myself any longer. I have experienced Oneness with the Divine. There is no doubt in my mind. I have nothing to fear. I have experienced Nirvana. I have experienced Christ Consciousness. I have looked into the Eyes of God and have seen myself in his image. His creation has come full circle once again and it is indescribable. It transcends religion. It is Heaven on Earth; sheer and utter bliss. I live an enchanted life. I feel like my world sits in the palm of my hand. I love our mother earth as God loves it because what he has created is perfect and complete, lacking absolutely nothing. The Kingdom of Heaven is within but once actualized, it can be projected outward onto the physical plane, creating Heaven on Earth. It is so wonderful.

It's Time to Put the Stitching on the Back of That and Get Some Feedback

I have been writing my story along with my dreams with the intention of putting it all together into a book to hopefully inspire others. I have had a calling to do this for a very long time. I really did not know exactly how it was going to come about, I just knew it would.

I received the name of the book in a vision that gave me a sense of direction. I pulled together all my dreams into themes and sub-themes based on the lessons and Universal Truths the dreams inspired within me. I did not know how it would start or where it would end or how many pages it would be. What I did know is that what I had received needed to be shared, and with the volume of material I had, it could easily fill several books.

I could not escape the urgency with which spirit pressed me to write this book. It was as if humanity's future rested upon it. I needed to write the book as if it would be the only book I would ever publish. My heart and soul had to be contained in the pages of this book. It needed to kindle a passion in the heart of humanity. I wanted it to paint a complete picture of the wonders and amazements I have found in the dream state. It needed to entice people sufficiently to seek out their own inner counsel to bring them into their own awareness of their multi-dimensional essence. It had to prove, or provide a means by which to prove, "THERE IS A GOD." For me, it has done both.

I wondered how I would know when I had reached the end. I figured I would just keep writing and eventually it would be revealed to me. Well the revelation came.

Yesterday I had trouble remembering my dream. All I could remember was seeing my back naked. I remembered nothing more -- just my back.

In the afternoon I ran over to GNC to pick up some things I needed and as the guy was ringing my merchandise up he asked me if I knew how someone would go about getting a book published. He said he had been working on a book and had about 300 pages and needed help finding a publisher. "What a coincidence," I told him, "I too am working on a book and I too have approximately 300 pages or more."

He began sharing with me the story line of his book and I thought to myself, "Wow that is one good story line." I told him I had intended on self-publishing my book and I could photocopy the materials and share it with him to help him. I believed that in helping him, I would somehow help myself. I knew something out there was trying to tell me it was time but I still wasn't sure. That night I had a dream.

In this dream there is a business woman with black hair wearing a baby blue pant suit. I am part of a team working under her direction. She walks by and I assume she is going to ask me for input on the project. As she walks by, I ask her if she wants me to follow her into her office. She turns to me and says, "No, why would I need you? I already stitched the hole in my pants bottom, can't you see?" She then shows me her bottom where she apparently had a hole in the seat of her pant suit where she had applied a needle and thread.

In the Course of a Dream Emanuel for Love

The stitching is that of an amateur seamstress. I comment, "Don't you think you could benefit from some professional feedback?" "No," she replies, "I did it myself."

That confirmed it was time to stitch up the pieces on this baby and get some honest feedback on how it looked and possibly seek out an editor and literary agent who knows how to sell and market a book.

I took a sigh of relief knowing it was a job well done. I laid in bed and meditated. I began hearing a tune along with the lyrics in my head of a song I had not heard in ages. The song was by Dee-Lite, *"Groove Is In The Heart."*

I meditated on the lyrics as they played in my head. I then had an out of body experience where I felt myself traveling our solar system. I flew by Mars, Jupiter, Saturn, Uranus, Neptune and Pluto. I continued on past other solar systems and galaxies. Far, far out into space I went, past beautiful clusters of stars and various nebulae.

My consciousness then came in and orbited a planet somewhere in the outer reaches of the universe. I circled the planet a number of times and slowly began my descent into the planet's atmosphere. I sped across its beautiful landscape and came to an inhabited city where people were walking to and fro.

My consciousness zoomed in on one fellow walking along a road toward me. He was in his late 30's with blond hair, wearing a tan colored shirt and khaki green colored pants. In his right hand he carried what looked to be a briefcase. He looked completely human. As he passed me on the street, he perceived me with curiosity and in recognition he smiled. A sense of knowing came over him and he was filled with what I could only describe as the Holy Ghost:

THE LAND OF CANAAN

"...my succotash wish.
DJ Soul (soul) was on a roll
I've been told he can't be sold
He's not vicious or malicious
Just de-lovely and delicious"[2]

I opened my eyes as goosebumps ran down my arms and back.

I got ready for work and left the house. Today was a special day. Instead of riding the train, I decided I would treat myself and drive in to work. I got in my car, turned the ignition key and when the radio came on I heard:

"We're going to dance,
We're going to dance,
We're going to dance
And have some fun

The chills that you
Spill up my back
Keep me filled with
Satisfaction when we're done
Satisfaction of what's to come"[3]

Believe it or not, Dee-Lite was playing on the radio. The song had just started the moment I turned the ignition key. It was not even a song that this particular radio station would typically play. I listen to the same station every

---

[2] Lyrics by Dee-Lite, *Groove Is In The Heart*, Album: *World Clique, 1990*

[3] Lyrics by Dee-Lite, *Groove Is In The Heart*, Album: *World Clique, 1990*

day and I had not heard the song in probably 15 years or more. Why today? The words were so applicable to what I was feeling within my heart. I remembered the lyrics back in the days when the song first came out.

I heard the soul of the universe sing its song to me in synchronous fashion as it has done with every penny it has placed in my path at precisely the right place, at the right time, to let me know I am on the right track.

I believe there is life out there in the universe and they too are endowed with the same spirit, the holiest of holies, the spirit of my Lord and Savior Jesus Christ who has come knocking on my door. God is the fabric that permeates all existence no matter what religion we claim for ourselves. God is ONE. I believe in Christ, in the Buddha, in Krishna, in the Tao and so many others. AMEN, MY LORD, for all who have come before me to guide the way. AMEN, MY LORD, AMEN.

The groove truly is in the heart. It is the path that leads directly to God and You. Let the penny guide you. I followed it and it led me home.

www.ingramcontent.com/pod-product-compliance
Lightning Source LLC
LaVergne TN
LVHW011346080426
835511LV00005B/145